The
Pennsylvania
Cookbook

Favorite Hometown Recipes from The Keystone State

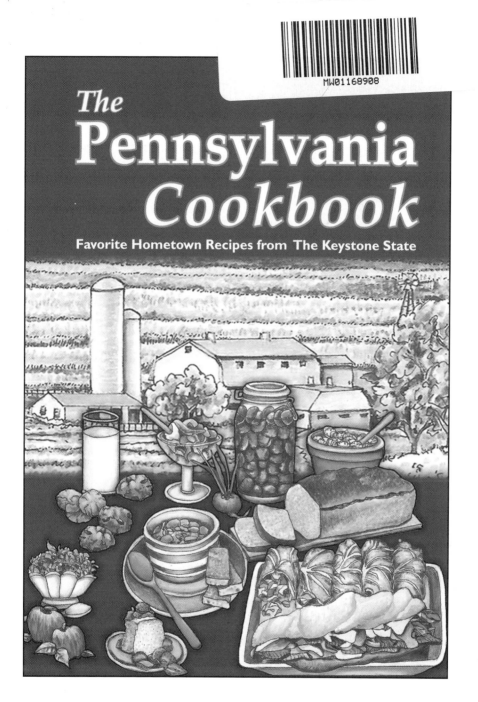

Cookbook Resources LLC
Highland Village, Texas

The Pennsylvania Cookbook
Favorite Hometown Recipes from The Keystone State

1ˢᵗ Printing - June 2009

International Standard Book Number: 978-1-59769-017-1

Library of Congress Control Number: 2008055171

Library of Congress Cataloging-in-Publication Data

    The Pennsylvania cookbook : favorite hometown recipes from the keystone state.
       p. cm.
    Includes bibliographical references and index.
    ISBN 978-1-59769-017-1
    1. Cookery--Pennsylvania. 2. Mennonite cookery. 3. Pennsylvania Dutch. I. Title.

    TX721.P327 2008
    641.59748--dc22

                            2008055171

Cover by Nancy Murphy Griffith

Manufactured in China and
Edited, Designed and Published in the United States of America by
Cookbook Resources, LLC
541 Doubletree Drive
Highland Village, Texas 75077

Toll free 866-229-2665

www.cookbookresources.com

Bringing Family and Friends to the Table

Welcome to Pennsylvania

What makes Pennsylvania the "Keystone State"? Many believe the nickname refers to the key role Pennsylvania played in the early history of the United States.

One of the original 13 colonies which became the United States, Pennsylvania was founded as a proprietary colony by William Penn who received a charter in 1681 in payment of a debt owed to his father by King Charles II of England. The colony is named for Penn's father, Admiral Sir William Penn. Persecuted and imprisoned in England for his faith as a Quaker, Penn looked to North America where he could found a settlement with freedom of religion for every faith. Pennsylvania became a haven for many who had been persecuted in their native Europe.

It was in Philadelphia that the Continental Congress met and signed the Declaration of Independence in 1776; Philadelphia was the first capital of the United States. This city was home to the development of the United States Constitution, in which Pennsylvania played a leading role. Pennsylvania was the second state to ratify this foundation document upon which our government and nation are based.

Pennsylvania has a strong history of championing worthwhile causes from William Penn's fair dealings with Native Americans, to abolition of slavery (the first state to pass a law providing for gradual emancipation), to major industrial leaders like Milton Hershey and H.J. Heinz who believed in just treatment and good environment for their workers.

Pennsylvania has a rich agricultural heritage celebrated in county fairs throughout the summer and fall. Agriculture is the number one industry in this largely rural state. From the peaceful farms of the Amish and Mennonites in and around Lancaster County to the rugged Allegheny Mountains that cross the state, Pennsylvania is filled with natural beauty. Its busy cities offer many cultural attractions as well as commercial enterprises with roots going back to dynamic industrial and financial giants like Andrew Carnegie, Charles M. Schwab, Henry Frick and Andrew Mellon who enriched Pennsylvania with their philanthropy.

With a history dating back to the 17th century, with scenic wonders from the rivers and streams to the mountains, and with fascinating areas like the Pennsylvania Dutch Country, Pennsylvania is a great place to visit – and a truly wonderful place to live.

Pennsylvania Cookery

The number one industry in Pennsylvania is agriculture – and Pennsylvania's rich and diverse cookery reflects on the many farms and variety of crops. Some of the best farmland in the United States is in the area of Lancaster County, Pennsylvania where Old Order Amish and Mennonites work the soil in traditional ways using horses to plow and harvest. Their farms are among the most productive in the country.

The diversity of Pennsylvania contributes greatly to its regional tastes. Influences from Native Americans, Swedish, Dutch, German and British settlers; later immigrants from many other ethnic groups; plus the distinctive tastes of the Amish and Mennonites have together created a delicious and unique cuisine including regional favorites from shoo-fly pie to scrapple.

With milk as the official state beverage, it's no surprise that Pennsylvania is the fourth largest state in dairy production. It is first in production of mushrooms. Other major crops include apples, cherries, peaches and grapes as well as field crops of winter wheat, buckwheat, potatoes, oats, rye, barley and a variety of vegetables. In addition, Pennsylvanian farms produce beef cattle, hogs, poultry and sheep. And there's a strong history of hunting and fishing. All of these enrich the tables of Pennsylvanian families.

Pennsylvania abounds with county fairs throughout the summer and fall. These celebrate the deep and continuing agricultural heritage of Pennsylvania with cooking and baking contests, livestock competitions, tractor pulls and much more including live entertainment, kids' activities, harness racing, demolition derbies and other events. Angel food cakes, apple pies and, of course, baking with Hershey's chocolate products are customary competitions at fairs – often followed by an old-fashioned baked goods auction. Many fairs have histories dating back more than 100 years. Nearly every county in Pennsylvania has a great fair, some lasting more than a week, with bushels of fun for every member of the family.

Enjoy the cooking traditions of Pennsylvania with delicious recipes from its rich rural heritage and from Pennsylvania Dutch to distinctive dishes influenced by the many nationalities who chose Pennsylvania as their home. We invite you to bring your family and friends to the table.

Map of Pennsylvania

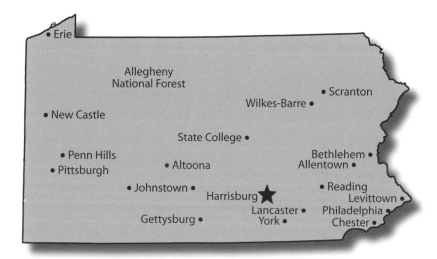

Dedication

With a mission of helping you bring family and friends to the table, Cookbook Resources strives to make family meals and entertaining friends simple, easy and delicious.

We recognize the importance of sharing meals as a means of building family bonds with memories and traditions that will be treasured for a lifetime. Mealtime is an opportunity to sit down with each other and share more than food.

This cookbook is dedicated with gratitude and respect for all those who show their love with homecooked meals, bringing family and friends to the table.

Contents

Appetizers .11

Beverages .19

Breakfast, Brunch and Breads. . . .25

Soups, Salads and Sandwiches . . .45

Vegetables and Side Dishes. 71

Contents

Pennsylvania
Food Festivals & Events

Month	Festival Name	Place
January	Pennsylvania Farm Show	Harrisburg
February	Groundhog Day (February 2)	Punxsutawney
March/April	Pennsylvania Maple Festival	Meyersdale
April	Pennsylvania Herb Festival	York
May	Strawberry Festival	Lahaska
	Pittsburgh Folk Festival	Pittsburgh
	Greek Food Festival	Pittsburgh
June	Schnecksville Community Fair	Schnecksville
	Northeast Fair	Northeast Fairgrounds
July	Black Cherry Festival	Kane
	Blueberry Festival	Bethlehem
	Lycoming County Fair	Hughesville
	Jacktown Fair	Wind Ridge
	Bedford County Fair	Bedford
	Troy Fair	Troy
	Fayette County Fair	Dunbar
July/August	Lebanon Area Fair	Lebanon
	Westmoreland Fair	Greensburg
August	Clinton County Fair	Mackeyville
	Washington County Agricultural Fair	Washington
	Lawrence County Fair	New Castle
	Pocono Garlic Festival	Stroudsburg
	Little League World Series	Williamsport

Pennsylvania
Food Festivals & Events

Month	Festival Name	Place
September	Chile Pepper Food Festival	Bowers
	Mushroom Festival	Kennett Square
	Pennsylvania Bavarian Oktoberfest	Canonsburg
	McClure Bean Soup Festival and Fair	McClure
	America's Oldest Agricultural Fair	York
October	Apple Cider Festival	Glendale
November	Apple Festival	Lahaska
December	Dickens of a Christmas	Wellsboro

With agriculture as Pennsylvania's leading industry, there are a multitude of county fairs and festivals throughout the summer and early autumn months. Nearly every one of Pennsylvania's 67 counties has an annual fair featuring exhibits of livestock, farm products and foods plus fun and entertainment. Many of these events last an entire week or more. Check local listings or the event's Web site for exact times and places.

Pennsylvania National Parks

Name	Location
Allegheny Portage Railroad National Historic Site	Gallitzin
Appalachian National Scenic Trail	14 States: Maine, New Hampshire, Vermont, Massachusetts, Connecticut, New York, New Jersey, Pennsylvania, Maryland, West Virginia, Virginia, Tennessee, North Carolina, Georgia
Delaware National Scenic River	Two States: New Jersey, Pennsylvania
Delaware Water Gap National Recreation Area	Bushkill
Edgar Allan Poe National Historic Site	Philadelphia
Eisenhower National Historic Site	Gettysburg
Flight 93 National Memorial	Somerset
Fort Necessity National Battlefield	Farmington
Friendship Hill National Historic Site	Point Marion
Gettysburg National Military Park	Gettysburg
Gloria Dei (Old Swedes' Church) National Historic Site	Philadelphia
Hopewell Furnace National Historic Site	Elverson
Independence National Historical Park	Philadelphia
Johnstown Flood National Memorial	South Fork
Potomac Heritage National Scenic Trail	Three States: Virginia, Maryland, Pennsylvania, District of Columbia
Steamtown National Historic Site	Scranton
Thaddeus Kosciuszko National Memorial	Philadelphia
Upper Delaware Scenic and Recreational River	Two States: Pennsylvania, New York
Valley Forge National Historical Park	King of Prussia

Appetizers

Dips
Finger Foods
Relishes

State Capital: *Harrisburg*

State Nickname: *The Keystone State*

State Motto: *Virtue, Liberty and Independence*

Pickled Beets

6 beets with stems
½ cup vinegar
½ cup sugar
6 whole peppercorns

- Cut stems about 3 inches above top of beets. Place in large saucepan with enough water to cover and cook over medium-high heat until tender. Drain beets and set aside beet juice.

- Peel and slice beets when cool and place in saucepan. Pour 1 cup beet juice over beets. Add vinegar, sugar and a dash of salt and cook just enough to get hot. Add peppercorns to pint or quart jars and pour in beets with juice while hot. Seal lids and store until ready to serve. If jars do not "seal", place jars in refrigerator until ready to serve. Serves 10 to 12.

Pickled Okra

1 quart young tender pods fresh okra
4 cups white vinegar
1 clove garlic

- Pack okra in sterilized jars.

- Combine vinegar, 1 cup water, ⅓ cup salt and garlic in saucepan and bring to a boil. Reduce heat and simmer for about 10 minutes.

- Pour over okra and seal jars. Store for 2 to 3 weeks before serving. Serves 6 to 10.

Simple Simon's Pickled Eggs

3 eggs, hard-boiled
Pickle juice (juice saved from a jar of pickles)

- Place eggs in pint jar. Pour in pickle juice to fill jar; seal with lid. Refrigerate for 5 days before serving. Yields 3 eggs.

Oma's Pickled Eggs

1 dozen eggs
1 cup pickled beet juice*
1 cup malt or cider vinegar
1 - 2 cloves garlic
2 teaspoons pickling spice
I medium sweet onion

- Place each egg carefully in large pot and cover with water. Cover pot and bring to a boil.

- Remove pot from heat and set aside for 10 to 15 minutes.

- Drain hot water; add cold water and ice cubes. Allow eggs to cool.

- Mix beet juice, vinegar, garlic, picking spice, 4 cups water and ½ teaspoon salt in a 1-gallon jar; mix well.

- Slice onion and separate into rings. Alternate eggs and onion rings in jar with liquid; seal with lid.

- Refrigerate for 5 to 7 days before serving. Yields 1 dozen eggs.

TIP: If you can't find beet juice, buy canned pickled beets and use juice from can.

Everyday Corn Relish

2 heads cabbage, minced
12 ears corn-on-the-cob
4 red bell peppers, seeded, chopped
3 large onions, chopped
1 cup sugar
2 cups vinegar

- Place cabbage in large saucepan. Cut corn off cob and add to cabbage. Add bell peppers and onions and mix. Add enough water to barely cover and cook on high heat until cabbage is just tender. Drain well and place in glass container.

- In separate bowl mix sugar, vinegar and 1 to 2 tablespoons salt and stir well. Pour over cabbage and corn, cover and refrigerate. Stir occasionally. Serves 12 to 14.

Tomato Relish

2 cups chopped tomato
1 cup chopped yellow tomato
½ cup finely chopped cucumber, peeled, seeded
½ cup finely chopped green bell pepper
½ cup finely chopped red onion
3 tablespoons chopped fresh basil
2 tablespoons lime juice
½ teaspoon sugar
½ teaspoon cayenne pepper

- Drain chopped vegetables. Mix all ingredients and ½ teaspoon salt in bowl. Cover and refrigerate. Serve as a salsa or with meat or vegetables. Yields 1 quart.

Spicy Party Spread

1 cup chopped pecans
1 tablespoon butter, melted
2 (8 ounce) packages cream cheese, softened
1 (1 ounce) packet taco seasoning
⅔ cup shredded cheddar cheese
1 cup picante sauce
1 bunch green onions with tops, chopped
Crackers

- Preheat oven to 275° (135° C).

- Bake pecans in shallow pan with butter for about 25 minutes.

- Use mixer to beat together cream cheese, taco seasoning and cheddar cheese. Stir in picante sauce, pecans and green onions.

- Spoon into sprayed 9-inch glass pie pan.

- Bake covered for 15 minutes. Serve hot and spread on crackers.

The Pennsylvania Herb Festival is held annually in York, Pennsylvania usually in April. This two-day event celebrates herbs, food and crafts.

Cocky Broccoli Cheese Dip

1 (10 ounce) package frozen chopped broccoli, thawed, drained
2 tablespoons butter
2 ribs celery, chopped
1 small onion, finely chopped
1 (1 pound) box mild Mexican Velveeta® cheese, cubed

- Make sure broccoli is thoroughly thawed and drained.
  (Squeeze between paper towels to completely remove
  excess moisture.)

- Place butter in large saucepan and saute broccoli, celery and
  onion on medium heat for about 5 minutes; stir several times.

- Add cheese and heat and stir just until cheese melts. Serve hot
  with chips.

Apple Butter Dip

1 (8 ounce) package cream cheese
½ cup apple butter
¼ cup packed brown sugar
½ teaspoon vanilla
½ cup chopped peanuts
Apples, cored, sliced

- Combine cream cheese, apple butter, brown sugar and vanilla
  in mixing bowl. Beat until smooth.

- Stir in peanuts; refrigerate. Serve with apple slices.

*The Pennsylvania Farm Show is held annually in Harrisburg
for one week in January. It is the largest indoor agricultural
event in the nation and averages over 400,000 visitors annually
with 8,000 exhibitors, 6,000 animals and numerous shows and
competitions such as Best Chef in Pennsylvania.*

Easy Baked Mozzarella Sticks

1 egg
½ cup Italian-seasoned breadcrumbs
1 (12 ounce) package mozzarella string cheese
Marinara sauce

- Preheat oven to 350º.

- Beat egg until foamy in shallow bowl.

- In small skillet, cook breadcrumbs over medium heat until light brown, about 5 minutes.

- Dip cheese in egg, then coat completely with breadcrumbs. Place on sprayed, foil-lined baking sheet. Lightly spray tops of cheese sticks.

- Bake for 5 to 6 minutes or until heated. Serve with warmed marinara sauce.

TIP: *If you don't have Italian-seasoned breadcrumbs, just add 1 teaspoon Italian herb seasoning to plain breadcrumbs before toasting.*

Cheese Strips

1 loaf thin-sliced bread
1 (8 ounce) package shredded cheddar cheese
6 slices bacon, fried, drained, crumbled
½ cup chopped onion
1 cup mayonnaise

- Preheat oven to 400°.

- Remove crust from bread.

- Combine cheese, bacon, onion and mayonnaise in bowl and spread on bread slices.

- Cut slices into 3 strips and place on cookie sheet.

- Bake for 10 minutes. Serves 8 to 12.

TIP: *For a special touch, sprinkle with ⅓ cup slivered toasted almonds.*

Koch Käse

(Quick Cook Cheese)

6 tablespoons butter
1 (16 ounce) carton cottage cheese
1 tablespoon flour
1 teaspoon baking soda
½ teaspoon caraway seeds
Crackers

- Stir butter into cottage cheese in double boiler. Stir in flour and baking soda and cook, while stirring, until ingredients become creamy. Add caraway seeds and stir. Serve warm or cold on crackers. Serves 4 to 6.

Special Stuffed Mushrooms

1 pound large fresh mushrooms
1 medium onion, chopped
½ cup (1 stick) butter, melted
1 cup seasoned breadcrumbs
2 tablespoons ketchup
½ cup precooked crumbled bacon pieces
1 cup sour cream
½ cup milk
Paprika

- Preheat oven to 400°.

- Wash and dry mushrooms. Remove and chop stems and set aside the caps for stuffing.

- In skillet, saute mushroom stems and onion in butter. Stir in breadcrumbs and cook, stirring constantly, for 2 minutes. Add 1½ teaspoons salt, ¼ teaspoon pepper and ketchup.

- Stuff mixture in mushroom caps and place stuffed mushrooms (stuffed side up) in sprayed shallow baking pan. Sprinkle with bacon pieces.

- Mix sour cream and milk together and pour over mushrooms. Sprinkle with paprika and bake for 20 to 25 minutes.

Garlic-Stuffed Mushrooms

1 tablespoon extra virgin olive oil
2 tablespoons butter
¾ cup Italian breadcrumbs
3 cloves garlic, peeled, minced
¼ teaspoon oregano
½ teaspoon seasoned salt
¼ teaspoon cracked black pepper
18 large mushrooms, stemmed

- Preheat oven to 400°.

- Heat olive oil and butter in skillet over medium heat. Add breadcrumbs, stir to coat and cook about 5 minutes.

- Add garlic, oregano, seasoned salt and fresh ground black pepper and saute until garlic is translucent.

- Stuff each mushroom with breadcrumb mixture and place stuffed side up in sprayed 9 x 13-inch baking pan. Bake for 20 minutes or until mushrooms are tender. Serve hot or at room temperature. Serves 10 to 12.

White mushrooms were first cultivated by Lewis Downing in Downington, Pennsylvania, in the early 1920's. By 1926 a recipe for cream of white mushroom soup was being circulated. Today, Pennsylvania is the largest producer of mushrooms in the U.S.

Beverages

Punches

Cider

Wine

Smoothies

State Song: *Pennsylvania*

State Beverage: *Milk*

State Cookie: *Chocolate Chip Cookie*

Sparkling Cranberry Punch

2 quarts cranberry juice cocktail
1 (6 ounce) can frozen lemonade concentrate, thawed
1 quart ginger ale, chilled
Red food coloring, optional
Ice ring for punch bowl

- Combine cranberry juice cocktail and lemonade concentrate in large pitcher and refrigerate.

- When ready to serve, pour cranberry mixture into punch bowl, add ginger ale and stir well. Serves 8 to 12.

TIP: *You can freeze an ice ring of water with red food coloring or freeze an ice ring of cranberry juice.*

Christmas Party Punch

The almond extract really gives this punch a special taste!

3 cups sugar
1 (6 ounce) package lemon gelatin
1 (6 ounce) can frozen orange juice concentrate, thawed
⅓ cup lemon juice
1 (46 ounce) can pineapple juice
3 tablespoons almond extract
2 quarts ginger ale, chilled

- Combine sugar and 1 quart water. Heat until sugar dissolves.

- Add gelatin and stir until it dissolves. Add fruit juices, 1½ quarts water and almond extract; refrigerate.

- When ready to serve, place in punch bowl and add chilled ginger ale. Serves 50.

Mocha Punch

4 cups brewed coffee
¼ cup sugar
4 cups milk
4 cups (2 pints) chocolate ice cream, softened

• Combine coffee and sugar; stir until sugar is dissolved. Refrigerate for 2 hours.

• Just before serving, pour into a punch bowl. Add milk, mix well. Top with scoops of ice cream and stir well.

Victorian Iced Tea

4 individual tea bags
¼ cup sugar
1 (11 ounce) can frozen cranberry-raspberry juice concentrate, thawed

• Place tea bags in teapot and add 4 cups boiling water. Cover and steep for 5 minutes. Remove and discard tea bags. Add sugar and stir until it dissolves. Refrigerate.

• Just before serving, combine cranberry-raspberry concentrate and 4 cups cold water in 2½-quart pitcher. Stir in tea and serve with ice cubes. Serves 24

Spiced Mulled Cider

¼ cup packed brown sugar
2 quarts apple cider
1 teaspoon whole allspice
1 teaspoon whole cloves
1 (3 inch) stick cinnamon
Whole nutmeg

• Mix brown sugar, apple cider and ¼ teaspoon salt in saucepan. Put spices in tea ball or cheesecloth sack and add to cider.

• Bring to a boil, reduce heat and simmer for about 15 to 20 minutes. Remove spices and serve hot. Serves about 10.

Winter-Spiced Cider

1 gallon apple cider
2 cups orange juice
¼ cup maple syrup
½ teaspoon lemon extract
5 cinnamon sticks
3 teaspoons whole cloves
½ teaspoon whole allspice

- Combine apple cider, orange juice, maple syrup and lemon extract in large roasting pan.

- Place cinnamon sticks, cloves and allspice in piece of cheesecloth. Bring up corners, tie with string to form bag and add to roasting pan.

- Cook over medium heat (do not boil) for 15 to 20 minutes. Discard spice bag. Serves 16 to 22.

Instant Cocoa Mix

1 (8 quart) box dry milk powder
1 (12 ounce) jar non-dairy creamer
1 (16 ounce) can instant chocolate-flavored drink mix
1¼ cups powdered sugar

- Combine all ingredients and store in airtight container.

- To serve, use ¼ cup cocoa mix for each cup of hot water. Serves 48.

Usually held in early October at Prince Gallitzin State Park at Glendale, Pennsylvania, the annual Apple Cider Festival celebrates apple cider, apple butter and all things apple. A special feature is that only handmade arts and crafts are to be sold there.

Weinsaft

(Grape Juice)

5 pounds ripe grapes, washed
1 pound (2⅓ cups) sugar

- Heat grapes and 1 quart water in large saucepan over medium-high heat for about 5 minutes; strain through cheesecloth into separate saucepan.

- Add half sugar to juice and cook for about 15 minutes. Check sweetness about halfway through cooking process and add sugar if needed. Fill bottles and seal. Serves 4 to 6.

Betsy Ross Dandelion Wine

1 quart dandelion flower blossoms
2½ pounds sugar
½ yeast cake

- Boil dandelion blossoms in 1 gallon water for about 10 minutes and set aside to cool. Squeeze blossoms into juice and discard.

- Pour sugar and yeast cake into cooled juice. Let ferment until it stops. Strain slowly and pour into jars. Serves 2 to 4.

TIP: Cut 1 orange and ½ lemon into very thin slices and add to juice with sugar. Remove slices before pouring into jars.

Grapes are a significant agricultural product in Pennsylvania. The city of North East has the largest Welch's grape processing plant in the United States. There are some 100 wineries in the state.

Apple-Yogurt Smoothie

2 cups (1 pint) low-fat vanilla yogurt
1 Granny Smith apple, peeled, diced
½ cup orange juice
½ cup ice
2 tablespoons honey

- Mix all ingredients in blender and process until smooth.
  Serves 2.

TIP: Any kind of fruit will work with this combination.

Blueberry Smoothie

¾ cup blueberries (fresh or frozen)
1 (6 ounce) container vanilla or blueberry yogurt
½ cup crushed ice or 3 ice cubes

- Combine all ingredients in blender and blend until smooth.
  Serves 2

Peachy Peach Smoothie

2 cups peach nectar, chilled
1 (8 ounce) carton vanilla frozen yogurt
½ banana, sliced, chilled
1 (8 ounce) carton peach yogurt
1½ cups frozen peach slices, thawed

- Combine all ingredients in blender and blend until smooth.
  Serves 4.

*Located in the heart of northeastern Pennsylvania,
the Northeast Fairgrounds are situated between Wilkes-
Barre and Scranton adjacent to the Wilkes-Barre/Scranton
International Airport. The fair showcases agriculture,
horticulture, arts and crafts, and gardening along with food,
fun and much more every summer.*

Breakfast, Brunch and Breads

Geographic Center: *Centre, near Bellefonte*

Highest Point: *Mount Davis (3,213 feet)*

State Flagship: *United States Brig* Niagara

Overnight Breakfast

This is French toast the easy way and it's not just for company! The kids will love it too.

7 cups small cubes French bread, crust removed
¾ cup chopped pecans
1 (3 ounce) package cream cheese, softened
¼ cup sugar
1 (8 ounce) carton whipping cream
½ cup real maple syrup
6 eggs, slightly beaten
1 teaspoon vanilla
½ teaspoon ground cinnamon

- Place cubed bread in sprayed 9 x 13-inch baking dish and press down gently. Sprinkle with pecans.

- Beat cream cheese and sugar in bowl until fluffy and gradually mix in whipping cream and syrup.

- In separate bowl, whisk eggs, vanilla, cinnamon and ½ teaspoon salt and fold into cream cheese-whipping cream mixture. Slowly pour this mixture evenly over bread. Cover and refrigerate overnight.

- When ready to bake, preheat oven to 350°.

- Remove from refrigerator 20 minutes before baking.

- Cover and bake for 30 minutes or until center sets and top is golden brown.

- To serve, cut into squares and serve with maple syrup. Serves 8.

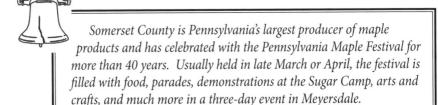

Somerset County is Pennsylvania's largest producer of maple products and has celebrated with the Pennsylvania Maple Festival for more than 40 years. Usually held in late March or April, the festival is filled with food, parades, demonstrations at the Sugar Camp, arts and crafts, and much more in a three-day event in Meyersdale.

Gigantic German Pancake

½ cup flour
3 eggs, slightly beaten
½ cup milk
2 tablespoons butter, melted
Powdered sugar
Maple syrup

- Preheat oven to 425°.

- Beat flour and eggs in bowl. Stir in milk, butter and ¼ teaspoon salt.

- Pour into sprayed 9-inch pie pan. Bake for 20 minutes. Pancake will puff into big bubbles while baking.

- Cut into wedges and dust with powdered sugar. Serve with melted butter and maple syrup. Serves 3 to 4.

Light, Crispy Waffles

2 cups biscuit mix
1 egg
½ cup canola oil
1⅓ cups club soda

- Preheat waffle iron. Combine all ingredients in bowl and stir with spoon. Pour just enough batter to cover waffle iron and cook

- To have waffles for a "company weekend", make up all waffles. Freeze separately on cookie sheet, place in large resealable bags.

- To heat, place in 350° oven for about 10 minutes. Serves 4.

Pennsylvania is designated as a "commonwealth" like Massachusetts, Virginia and Kentucky. It is a traditional description that is based on the old English usage of the common "weal" (well-being) of the people.

Orange French Toast

1 egg, beaten
½ cup orange juice
5 slices raisin bread
1 cup crushed graham crackers
2 tablespoons butter

- Combine egg and orange juice in bowl.

- Dip each slice of bread in egg mixture and then in graham cracker crumbs.

- Fry in butter in skillet until brown. Serves 5.

Old Days Cornmeal Waffles

2 large eggs
1 cup sour cream
1 cup buttermilk*
⅓ cup shortening, melted
1 cup flour
1 cup cornmeal
2 teaspoons baking powder
1 teaspoon baking soda

- Preheat waffle iron.

- Beat eggs well in large bowl. Add sour cream, buttermilk and shortening and mix well.

- In separate bowl, mix flour, cornmeal, baking powder and baking soda.

- Add dry ingredients to liquid mixture a little at a time and blend well.

- Spray waffle iron and pour just enough batter onto hot grill to just barely fill area.

- Cook for about 5 to 7 minutes and remove waffle when it reaches brown color.

- Serve with syrup and butter. Yields about 8 waffles.

*TIP: *To make buttermilk, mix 1 cup milk with 1 tablespoon lemon juice or vinegar and let stand for about 10 minutes.*

Easy Apple Butter

6 apples, peeled and finely chopped
½ cup apple cider
2 cups packed brown sugar
1½ teaspoon ground cinnamon
1 teaspoon ground nutmeg
½ teaspoon ground cloves

- Place apples and apple cider in 1½-quart microwaveable bowl. Cover tightly with plastic wrap. Microwave on HIGH for 6 minutes; remove plastic wrap and stir. Cover and microwave again on HIGH until apples are soft, about 6 to 7 minutes. Stir in brown sugar and spices. Microwave uncovered on HIGH for 3 minutes; stir and microwave until sugar melts.

- Process mixture in blender or food processor until smooth. Refrigerate. Yields 1 quart.

Apple Cider Syrup

This is great over pancakes.

1 cup apple cider or apple juice
1 tablespoon cornstarch
¾ cup sugar
1 tablespoon lemon juice
1 teaspoon ground cinnamon
½ teaspoon vanilla
2 tablespoons butter

- Combine apple cider and cornstarch in saucepan; stir continuously and cook over medium heat for several minutes.

- Continue stirring, reduce heat and add sugar, lemon juice, cinnamon and vanilla.

- Cook for about 3 to 4 minutes and remove from heat.

- Add butter and stir. Pour over waffles or pancakes while hot. Yields 1½ cups.

Apple Fritters

½ cup milk
2 eggs
1 cup flour
3 tablespoons sugar
¼ teaspoon ground cinnamon
1½ cups peeled, cored, chopped apples
Canola oil
Powdered sugar
Maple syrup

- Beat milk and eggs in small bowl. In separate bowl mix flour, sugar, cinnamon and a pinch of salt. Pour milk mixture into flour and stir well. Mix in apples.

- Heat oil to 365°. Drop batter by spoonfuls into hot oil. Fry until golden brown. Remove from hot oil and drain on paper towels.

- Before serving, sprinkle with powdered sugar. Serve with maple syrup. Serves 8 to 10.

Breakfast Cinnamon Cake

⅔ cup packed brown sugar
1 tablespoon grated orange peel
2 (12 ounce) packages refrigerated cinnamon rolls

- Preheat oven to 375°.

- Combine brown sugar and orange peel in small bowl. Open cans of rolls (save frosting), cut each in quarters and coat each with cooking spray.

- Dip in sugar-orange mixture and arrange evenly in sprayed, floured 10-inch bundt pan. Gently press down on each. Bake for 35 minutes until light brown and about double in size.

- Cool slightly in pan. Invert serving plate on top of pan, hold plate and pan together with oven mitts and invert. Remove pan. Spread frosting unevenly over top of cake and serve warm. Serves 6.

Old-Fashioned Blueberry Buckle

Excellent for brunch!

2 cups flour
3 cups sugar
2 teaspoons baking powder
1 egg
½ cup milk
¼ cup (½ stick) butter, softened
2 cups blueberries

- Preheat oven to 375°.

- Combine flour, sugar, baking powder, egg, ½ teaspoon salt, milk and butter in large bowl. Fold in blueberries carefully.

- Spread in sprayed, floured 9-inch square pan and set aside.

Topping:

¼ cup (½ stick) butter, softened
⅓ cup flour
½ cup sugar
½ teaspoon ground cinnamon

- Combine butter, flour, sugar and cinnamon in bowl and sprinkle over blueberry mixture

- Bake for 30 to 35 minutes. Serve warm. Serves 8 to 10.

The annual Blueberry Festival is held at Burnside Plantation, part of Historic Bethlehem, in Bethlehem, Pennsylvania in mid-summer. Buildings that were part of the original Moravian community date back to the 18th century. Burnside Plantation has many of the structures of a working farm of that era. This festival features authentic colonial crafts, baking contests, live music and much more.

Short-Cut Blueberry Coffee Cake

1 (16 ounce) package blueberry muffin mix
⅓ cup sour cream
1 egg
⅔ cup powdered sugar

- Preheat oven to 400°.

- Combine muffin mix, sour cream, egg and ½ cup water in bowl.
  Rinse blueberries from muffin mix and gently fold into batter.

- Pour into sprayed, floured 7 x 11-inch baking dish. Bake for about
  25 minutes and cool. Mix powdered sugar and 1 tablespoon water
  in bowl and drizzle over coffee cake. Serves 12.

Graham-Streusel Coffee Cake

2 cups graham cracker crumbs
¾ cup chopped pecans
¾ cup packed brown sugar
1½ teaspoons ground cinnamon
¾ cup (1½ sticks) butter, softened
1 (18 ounce) box yellow cake mix
½ cup canola oil
3 eggs

- Preheat oven to 350°.

- Mix graham cracker crumbs, pecans, brown sugar, cinnamon
  and butter in bowl and set aside. In separate bowl, blend cake
  mix, 1 cup water, oil and eggs on medium speed for 3 minutes.

- Pour half batter in sprayed, floured 9 x 13-inch baking pan.
  Sprinkle with half crumb mixture. Spread remaining batter
  evenly over crumb mixture. Sprinkle remaining crumb
  mixture over top. Bake for 45 to 50 minutes.

Glaze:

1½ cups powdered sugar

- Mix powdered sugar and 2 tablespoons water in bowl and
  drizzle over cake while still hot. Serves 8 to 10.

Brot

(Bread)

1 yeast cake
1 tablespoon shortening
1 tablespoon sugar
4 - 6 cups flour or enough to make a stiff dough

- Mix yeast, 1 quart warm water, shortening, sugar and 2 teaspoons salt in large bowl. Add enough flour to make stiff dough.

- Knead with hands for about 4 minutes, cover bowl with towel and let stand for 2 hours 30 minutes.

- Knead and punch down several times, cover bowl and let stand for 45 minutes.

- Divide into 4 equal balls and place in sprayed loaf pans. Set aside to rise until dough is above top of pans.

- When ready to bake, preheat oven to 325°. Bake for 1 hour. Yields 4 loaves.

Pennsylvania is not named for its founder, William Penn; it is named for his father, Admiral Sir William Penn. The Latin word "Sylvania" which means "woodlands" was Penn's original name for the colony, but King Charles II added the word "Penn". The name "Pennsylvania" was stated in the charter given to William Penn. So the name of the state translates as "Penn's Woods".

Knepp

Dumplings are a favorite that few make any more, but they are certainly part of the regional culinary tradition. Make this recipe when you are baking a ham. The seasonings in the ham's juices make the dish special.

2 cups flour
1 tablespoon baking powder
2 tablespoons butter, softened
1½ cups milk

- Mix flour, baking powder and ¼ teaspoon salt in bowl. Cut in butter until it is coarsely mixed.

- Place dough in blender and slowly pour in milk. Process just until lumps are gone and mixture is smooth.

- Pour juices (about 1½ cups) from freshly baked ham into saucepan. Add about ½ to 1 cup water and bring to a boil.

- Drop tablespoonfuls of dough in boiling liquid, cover and cook on low for about 10 to 12 minutes. Do not remove lid while cooking.

- Remove with slotted spoon, drain and serve hot. Serves 4 to 6.

McClure Bean Soup Festival and Fair is held annually in McClure, Pennsylvania as a living memorial to veterans of all wars. Local veterans of the Civil War began "Bean Soup" celebrations in the 1880's and began inviting the public in 1891 to sample real Civil War bean soup. Now, more than 75,000 people attend each year to enjoy bean soup made with tons of beans, a ton of beef and a ton of crackers. You can watch the soup being made in huge kettles over wood fires and have fun with the family with entertainment, rides, exhibits, Civil War reenactments and much more.

Sticky Buns

Try these for brunch or a morning get-together. Soft and fluffy, topped with caramel-coated pecans, they look and taste like they came straight from the bakery!

2 (.25 ounce) packages dry yeast
1 (18 ounce) box yellow cake mix
4 cups flour
½ cup butter, divided
2 tablespoons sugar
1 teaspoon ground cinnamon
¼ cup light corn syrup
¼ cup packed brown sugar
2 cups pecan halves

- Dissolve yeast in 2½ cups warm water and let stand for 10 minutes. Combine cake mix and flour in large bowl. Stir in yeast mixture and blend well. Cover bowl and let rise in warm place until doubled in size, about 1 hour.

- Roll dough on floured work surface into rectangle about ¼-inch thick (about 12 x 24 inch). Melt ¼ cup butter and spread over dough using pastry brush or back of spoon. Combine sugar and cinnamon in small bowl and sprinkle evenly over dough. Starting with longest side, roll dough into log.

- Combine corn syrup, brown sugar and remaining ¼ cup butter in small saucepan. Cook over low heat, stirring frequently, until butter melts and mixture is smooth. Pour evenly into sprayed 10 x 15-inch baking pan. Sprinkle pecans evenly.

- Slice dough into 1½ to 2-inch pieces and place close together (flat-side down) over pecans in pan. Cover with plastic wrap and let rise again until doubled in size, about 30 minutes.

- When ready to bake, preheat oven to 350°.

- Bake for 25 minutes or until toothpick inserted halfway in center comes out clean. Remove from oven, let stand for 2 to 3 minutes, then unmold onto serving tray. Cool slightly and serve warm or cold. Yields about 20 rolls.

Applesauce-Pecan Bread

1 cup sugar
1 cup applesauce
⅓ cup canola oil
2 eggs
2 tablespoons milk
1 teaspoon almond extract
2 cups flour
1 teaspoon baking soda
½ teaspoon baking powder
¾ teaspoon ground cinnamon
¼ teaspoon ground nutmeg
¾ cup chopped pecans

- Preheat oven to 350°.

- Combine sugar, applesauce, oil, eggs, milk and almond extract in bowl and mix well.

- In separate bowl, combine all dry ingredients and ¼ teaspoon salt; add to sugar mixture and mix well. Fold in pecans. Pour into sprayed, floured loaf pan.

Topping:

½ cup chopped pecans
½ teaspoon ground cinnamon
½ cup packed brown sugar

- Combine pecans, cinnamon and brown sugar in bowl. Sprinkle over batter.

- Bake for 1 hour 5 minutes. Bread is done when toothpick inserted in center comes out clean. Cool on rack. Serves 12.

Pennsylvania became the second state December 12, 1787, because it was the second of the original 13 colonies to ratify the Constitution of the United States.

Sweet Apple Loaf

⅔ cup (1⅓ sticks) butter
2 cups sugar
4 eggs
2 cups applesauce
⅓ cup milk
1 tablespoon lemon juice
4 cups flour
1 teaspoon ground cinnamon
2 teaspoons baking powder
1 teaspoon baking soda
1½ cups chopped pecans
¾ cup chopped maraschino cherries, well drained

- Preheat oven to 325° (160° C).

- Cream butter, sugar and eggs in bowl and beat for several minutes. Stir in applesauce, milk and lemon juice.

- In separate bowl, sift flour, cinnamon, baking powder, baking soda and 1 teaspoon (5 ml) salt, add to first mixture and mix well. Fold in pecans and cherries.

- Pour into 3 sprayed, floured loaf pans and bake for 1 hour. Bread is done when toothpick inserted in center comes out clean. Set aside for 10 to 15 minutes, remove from pans and cool on rack. Freezes well. Serve toasted for breakfast or spread with cream cheese for lunch. Serves 18.

Quick Pumpkin Bread

1 (16 ounce) package pound cake mix
1 cup canned pumpkin
2 eggs
⅓ cup milk
1 teaspoon allspice

- Preheat oven to 350°.

- Beat all ingredients in bowl and blend well. Pour into sprayed, floured 9 x 5-inch loaf pan.

- Bake for 1 hour. Bread is done when toothpick inserted in center comes out clean.

- Cool and turn out onto cooling rack. Serves 15.

Mom's Quick Never-Fail Bread

This whole process takes less than 5 hours.

1½ yeast cakes
½ cup milk, room temperature
1 tablespoon sugar
2 tablespoons butter, melted
5 - 6 cups flour

- Dissolve yeast in 1½ cups warm water and warm milk in large bowl.

- Mix in sugar, 1½ teaspoons salt and butter until it blends well.

- Slowly pour flour into mixture and stir after each addition. Add flour until dough is stiff enough to knead.

- Place on lightly floured board and knead until dough is smooth and springs back when touched.

- Cover and set aside in warm place until dough doubles in size. Punch down lightly and divide into 2 equal parts.

- Place in sprayed, floured loaf pans, cover and let stand in warm place until dough doubles in size again.

- When ready to bake, preheat oven to 450°.

- Bake for 15 minutes. Reduce heat to 350° and bake for 30 minutes or until golden brown on top. Yields 2 loaves.

Agriculture is a primary industry in Pennsylvania, including dairy products, poultry, cattle, nursery stock, mushrooms, hogs and hay as well as fruit and vegetables.

Very Berry Strawberry Bread

3 cups sifted flour
2 cups sugar
1 teaspoon baking soda
1 tablespoon ground cinnamon
3 large eggs, beaten
1 cup canola oil
1¼ cups pecans, chopped
2 (10 ounce) packages frozen sweetened strawberries, thawed
1 (8 ounce) package light cream cheese, softened

- Preheat oven to 350°.

- Combine flour, sugar, 1 teaspoon salt, baking soda and cinnamon in large bowl.

- Add remaining ingredients except cream cheese.

- Pour in 2 sprayed, floured 9 x 5-inch loaf pans.

- Bake for 1 hour or until toothpick inserted in center comes out clean.

- Cool for several minutes before removing from pan.

- To serve, slice bread and spread cream cheese between 2 slices. For finger sandwiches, cut in smaller pieces. Serves 12 to 16.

Enjoy strawberry fritters, strawberry jam, strawberries dipped in chocolate, strawberry pastries and more at the Strawberry Festival. This two-day event is held in the spring in Lahaska, Pennsylvania and features live entertainment, strawberry pie-eating contests and lots of fresh strawberries.

Zucchini-Pineapple Bread

3 eggs, beaten
2 cups sugar
1 cup canola oil
2 teaspoons vanilla
2 cups grated zucchini
3 cups flour
1 teaspoon baking soda
1 teaspoon ground cinnamon
½ teaspoon baking powder
1 cup chopped pecans
1 (8 ounce) can crushed pineapple, drained
1 (8 ounce) carton spreadable cream cheese

- Preheat oven to 325°.

- Mix eggs, sugar, oil and vanilla in bowl and mix well.

- Add remaining ingredients (except cream cheese) and
  1 teaspoon salt, mix well and pour in 2 sprayed, floured
  9 x 5-inch loaf pans.

- Bake for 60 minutes or until toothpick inserted in center comes
  out clean. Cool for several minutes.

- To serve, slice and spread with cream cheese. Serves 12 to 16.

*Jimmy Stewart (1908-1997) was born James Maitland
Stewart in Indiana, Pennsylvania. An Academy Award-
winning actor for* The Philadelphia Story, *he starred in a
number of classic movies and was nominated for five Oscars. The
Jimmy Stewart Museum is located in his hometown which also
features a statue of Stewart on the courthouse lawn. Every year
at Christmastime, the downtown area of Indiana is decorated
with the theme of his famous movie,* It's a Wonderful Life.

Apple-Spice Muffins

1 cup (2 sticks) butter, softened
1 cup packed brown sugar
1 cup sugar
2 eggs
1¾ cups applesauce
2 teaspoons ground cinnamon
1 teaspoon ground allspice
½ teaspoon ground cloves
2 teaspoons baking soda
3½ cups flour
1½ cups chopped pecans

- Preheat oven to 375°.

- Cream butter, brown sugar and sugar in bowl.

- Add eggs, applesauce, cinnamon, allspice, cloves, ½ teaspoon salt, baking soda and flour and mix well. Add pecans and stir well.

- Pour into 28 sprayed, floured muffin cups (or cups with paper liners).

- Bake for 16 minutes or until toothpick inserted in center comes out clean. Serves 28.

Built between 1732 and 1756, Independence Hall in Philadelphia was first known as the Statehouse for the colony of Pennsylvania. It is considered an excellent example of Georgian architecture. It was the meeting place of the Second Continental Congress from 1775-1783 except for the winter of 1777-1778 when the British occupied Philadelphia. It was here that George Washington was appointed commander-in-chief of the Continental Army in 1775 and the Declaration of Independence was adopted July 4, 1776. The Articles of Confederation (the precursor to the Constitution) were adopted there in 1781 and the U.S. Constitution was drafted in 1787. The building has been restored to its late 18th century appearance.

Fresh Blueberry Muffins

1¼ cups sugar
2 cups flour
1½ teaspoons baking powder
½ cup (1 stick) butter, softened
1 egg, beaten
1 cup milk
1½ cups fresh blueberries
½ cup chopped pecans

- Preheat oven to 375°.

- Combine sugar, flour, baking powder and ½ teaspoon salt in large bowl. Cut in softened butter until mixture is coarse.

- Stir in egg and milk and beat well. Gently fold in blueberries and pecans, but do not beat.

- Spoon into sprayed, floured muffin cups (or cups with paper liners) and bake for 35 minutes or until light brown. Yields 12 muffins.

Ginger-Raisin Muffins

1 (18 ounce) box gingerbread mix
1 egg
2 (1.5 ounce) boxes seedless raisins

- Preheat oven to 350°.

- Combine gingerbread mix, 1¼ cups lukewarm water and egg in bowl and mix well. Stir in raisins.

- Pour into 12 sprayed, floured muffin cups (or cups with paper liners) until filled half full.

- Bake for 20 minutes or until toothpick inserted in center comes out clean. Serves 12.

Easy Brunch Biscuits

½ cup (1 stick) butter, melted
2 cups self-rising flour
1 (8 ounce) carton sour cream

- Preheat oven to 350°.

- Combine all ingredients in bowl and mix well. Spoon into sprayed miniature muffin cups (or cups with paper liners). Bake for 15 minutes or until light brown. Yields 8 biscuits.

TIP: These biscuits are so rich they do not need butter.

Farmhouse Cream Biscuits

2 cups flour
3 teaspoons baking powder
1 (8 ounce) carton whipping cream

- Preheat oven to 375°.

- Combine flour, baking powder and ½ teaspoon salt in bowl.

- In separate bowl, beat whipping cream only until it holds shape. Combine flour mixture and cream and mix with fork.

- Place dough on lightly floured board and knead it for about 1 minute. Pat dough to ¾-inch thickness. Cut out biscuits with small biscuit cutter. Place on sprayed baking sheet and bake for about 12 minutes or until light brown. Serves 6 to 8.

Everyday Butter Rolls

2 cups biscuit mix
1 (8 ounce) carton sour cream
½ cup (1 stick) butter, melted

- Preheat oven to 400°.

- Combine all ingredients in bowl and mix well. Spoon into 8 sprayed muffin cups (or cups with paper liners) and fill only half full. Bake for 12 to 14 minutes or light brown. Serves 6 to 8.

Spatzle

This traditional dish is a sort of dumpling-noodle.

1½ cups flour
2 eggs, beaten
½ cup milk
Canola oil

- Mix flour and eggs in large bowl. Add milk, a little at a time, and beat until dough is smooth.

- Add 1 teaspoon salt and a dash of oil to 1 quart water in saucepan and bring to a boil.

- Press dough through a colander or spatzle maker and drop pieces into boiling water. Cook until pieces float on surface.

- Remove with slotted spoon and serve immediately. Serves 4 to 6.

TIP   You can serve spatzle plain with a little butter or with a dash of nutmeg for added flavor.

Mama's Corn Fritters

1 tablespoon baking powder
1½ cups flour
½ teaspoon sugar
1 egg, beaten
1 (8 ounce) can whole kernel corn, drained
Milk
Canola oil

- Sift dry ingredients plus ½ teaspoon salt in bowl and add egg, corn and only enough milk to make batter consistency.

- Mix well and drop tablespoonfuls of batter in hot oil and fry until golden brown. Yields about 2 dozen fritters.

Soups, Salads and Sandwiches

State Dog: *Great Dane*

State Fossil: *Trilobite*

State Insect: *Firefly*

Strawberry Soup

1½ cups fresh strawberries
1 cup orange juice
¼ cup honey
½ cup sour cream
½ cup white wine

- Combine all ingredients in blender and puree.

- Chill thoroughly. Stir before serving. Serves 2.

Incredible Broccoli-Cheese Soup

Everyone will want seconds and thirds because this soup is so rich and flavorful.

1 (10 ounce) box frozen chopped broccoli
3 tablespoons butter
½ onion, finely chopped
¼ cup flour
1 (16 ounce) carton half-and-half cream
1 (14 ounce) can chicken broth
⅛ teaspoon cayenne pepper
1 (16 ounce) package cubed, mild Mexican Velveeta® cheese

- Punch several holes in box of broccoli and microwave on HIGH for 5 minutes. Rotate box in microwave and cook on HIGH for additional 4 minutes. Leave in microwave for 3 minutes.

- Melt butter in large saucepan and cook onion until it is translucent. Add flour and stir. Gradually add half-and-half cream, chicken broth, ½ teaspoon salt and cayenne pepper and stir constantly.

- Heat until mixture thickens. Do not boil. Add cheese and stir constantly until cheese melts. Add cooked broccoli and serve hot. Serves 6.

Chicken-Corn Soup with Rivels

Rivels are like tiny little dumplings made by crumbling the dough into the boiling liquid.

2 pounds cut-up chicken
5 cups water
1 medium onion, chopped
½ cup chopped celery
2 tablespoons chopped parsley
1 cup flour
1 egg beaten,
¼ cup milk
1 (15 ounce) can whole kernel corn

- Cook chicken in boiling water until meat is ready to fall off the bones; remove skin and bones. Chop chicken meat and set aside.

- Strain the stock and return to pot. Add onion and celery and simmer until vegetables are tender. Add parsley and a little salt and pepper.

- Mix flour, egg and milk with fork until mixture forms crumbs. Use your hands to drop crumbs slowly into simmering soup, cover and cook for 10 minutes.

- Add chicken and corn and cook for additional 5 minutes until thoroughly hot. Serves 3 to 4.

Easy Potato Soup

1 (18 ounce) package frozen hash-brown potatoes
1 cup chopped onion
1 (14 ounce) can chicken broth
1 (10 ounce) can cream of celery soup
1 (10 ounce) can cream of chicken soup
2 cups milk

- Combine potatoes, onion and 2 cups water in large saucepan and bring to a boil.

- Cover, reduce heat and simmer for 30 minutes.

- Stir in broth, soups and milk and heat thoroughly. Serves 6.

TIP: If you like, garnish with shredded cheddar cheese or cooked, diced ham.

Cabbage and Potato Soup

4 cups coarsely shredded cabbage
2 medium potatoes, peeled, chopped
1 cup chopped onion
2 (15 ounce) cans diced tomatoes
3 tablespoons lemon juice
2 tablespoons plus 2 teaspoons sugar
¼ teaspoon dried thyme

- Combine cabbage, potatoes, onion and 3 cups water in soup pot.

- Cover and cook on medium heat for 15 minutes.

- Add remaining ingredients. Bring to a boil. Cover and reduce heat to low.

- Simmer for 45 minutes to 1 hour or until potatoes are tender. Serves 4 to 6.

Potato-Sausage Soup

1 pound pork sausage links
1 cup chopped celery
1 cup chopped onion
2 (10 ounce) cans potato soup
2 (14 ounce) cans chicken broth

- Cut sausage in 1-inch slices.

- Brown sausage slices in large heavy skillet, drain and remove sausage to separate bowl.

- Leave about 2 tablespoons sausage drippings in skillet and saute celery and onion.

- Add soup, ¾ cup water, broth and cooked sausage slices.

- Bring to a boil, reduce heat and simmer for 20 minutes. Serves 6.

Potato-Spinach Soup

3 large potatoes, peeled, chopped
½ cup chopped onion
¼ cup (½ stick) butter
3 cups chicken broth
1 quart chopped fresh spinach
3 cups milk

- Cook potatoes and onions in large pot with butter, stir until potatoes are slightly golden.

- Add chicken broth and 1 quart water; cook over medium-high heat until potatoes are tender enough to mash. Mash potatoes in pot.

- Add spinach and cook just until tender. Add milk and a little salt and pepper, mix well and bring to a boil. Remove from heat and serve hot. Serves 6 to 8.

Homemade Tomato Soup

3 (15 ounce) cans whole tomatoes
1 (14 ounce) can chicken broth
1 tablespoon sugar
1 tablespoon minced garlic
1 tablespoon balsamic vinegar
¾ cup whipping cream

- Puree tomatoes with liquid in blender (in batches) and pour into large saucepan.

- Add chicken broth, sugar, garlic, balsamic vinegar and a little salt and bring to a boil. Reduce heat and stir in whipping cream.

- Cook, stirring constantly for 2 to 3 minutes or until soup is thoroughly hot. Serves 4 to 6.

TIP: *You might want to garnish each serving with 1 tablespoon ready-cooked, crumbled bacon.*

Fast Lentil Soup

2 cups lentils
1 small Irish potato, peeled, cubed
2 ribs celery, chopped
1 onion, chopped
¼ cup (½ stick) butter

- Soak lentils overnight in enough water to cover. Drain lentils and place in large pot with 3 quarts water.

- Add potato, celery, onion and butter. Cook slowly over medium-low heat until potato and onion are tender. Serves 4 to 5.

Rainy Day Lentil Soup

¼ cup apple juice
1 cup chopped onions
½ cup diced celery
2 (14 ounce) cans chicken broth
1 cup shredded carrots
½ cup shredded sweet potatoes
1 cup dry lentils, sorted, rinsed
1 - 2 tablespoons minced garlic
½ teaspoon cumin

- Bring apple juice to a boil in large saucepan. Add onions and celery and return to boil.

- Add chicken broth, carrots, sweet potatoes, lentils and garlic and bring to a boil.

- Reduce heat to medium and add cumin. Cover and cook for about 30 minutes or until flavors blend. Add a little salt and pepper. Serves 4.

Held in late summer or early fall, the Pocono Garlic Festival features the renowned garlic grown in the Poconos as well as great food and entertainment in a two-day event at Shawnee-on-Delaware near Stroudsburg, Pennsylvania.

Spicy Bean Soup

1 cup dried great northern beans
1 ham hock
2 chorizo sausages
1 onion, chopped
½ teaspoon cayenne pepper
1 large potato, peeled, cubed
1 bunch turnip greens, finely shredded

- Boil beans in 2½ quarts water in large saucepan for 2 minutes. Remove from heat and soak for 1 hour.

- Add ham hock and bring to a boil. Lower heat and simmer for 1 hour 30 minutes.

- Prick sausages with fork. Add onion, 2 teaspoons salt, cayenne pepper, potato and sausages. Simmer for 30 minutes. Add turnip greens and cook on low for additional 15 minutes. Serves 6.

Everyday Hamburger Soup

2 pounds lean ground beef
2 (15 ounce) cans chili without beans
1 (16 ounce) package frozen mixed vegetables, thawed
3 (14 ounce) cans beef broth
2 (15 ounce) cans stewed tomatoes

- Brown ground beef in skillet and place in 6-quart slow cooker.

- Add chili, vegetables, broth, tomatoes, 1 cup water and 1 teaspoon salt and stir well. Cover and cook on LOW for 6 to 7 hours. Serves 6.

Among the original specialty foods that Pennsylvania has shared with the nation are scrapple, cheese steaks, shoo-fly pie and funnel cakes.

Beefy Noodle Soup

1 pound beef round steak, cubed
1 onion, chopped
2 ribs celery, sliced
1 tablespoon canola oil
1 tablespoon chili powder
½ teaspoon dried oregano
1 (15 ounce) can stewed tomatoes
2 (14 ounce) cans beef broth
½ (8 ounce) package egg noodles
1 green bell pepper, seeded, chopped

- Cook and stir cubed steak, onion and celery in soup pot with oil for 15 minutes or until beef browns.

- Stir in 2 cups water, 1 teaspoon salt, chili powder, oregano, stewed tomatoes and beef broth.

- Bring to a boil, reduce heat and simmer for 1 hour 30 minutes to 2 hours or until beef is tender.

- Stir in noodles and bell pepper and heat to boiling. Reduce heat and simmer for 10 to 15 minutes or until noodles are tender. Serves 6 to 8.

Fast Chicken Noodle Soup

1 (3 ounce) package chicken-flavored ramen noodles, broken
1 (10 ounce) package frozen green peas, thawed
1 (4 ounce) jar sliced mushrooms, drained
3 cups cooked, cubed chicken

- Heat 2¼ cups water in large saucepan to boiling. Add ramen noodles, contents of seasoning packet and peas.

- Heat to boiling, reduce heat to medium and cook for about 5 minutes.

- Stir in mushrooms and chicken and continue cooking over low heat until all ingredients are hot. Serves 4 to 6.

Tasty Chicken and Rice Soup

1 pound boneless skinless chicken breasts
½ cup brown rice
1 (10 ounce) can cream of chicken soup
1 (10 ounce) can cream of celery soup
1 (14 ounce) can chicken broth with roasted garlic
1 (16 ounce) package frozen sliced carrots, thawed
1 cup half-and-half cream

- Cut chicken into 1-inch pieces.

- Place pieces in sprayed 4 to 5-quart slow cooker.

- Mix rice, soups, broth and carrots in bowl and pour over chicken.

- Cover and cook on LOW for 7 to 8 hours.

- Turn heat to HIGH, add half-and-half cream and cook for additional 15 to 20 minutes. Serves 6.

Spicy Turkey Soup

3 - 4 cups cooked, chopped turkey or chicken
3 (10 ounce) cans chicken broth
2 (10 ounce) cans diced tomatoes and green chilies
1 (15 ounce) can whole kernel corn
1 large onion, chopped
1 (10 ounce) can tomato soup
1 teaspoon garlic powder
1 teaspoon dried oregano
3 tablespoons cornstarch

- Combine turkey, broth, tomatoes and green chilies, corn, onion, tomato soup, garlic powder, and oregano in large roasting pan.

- Mix cornstarch with 3 tablespoons water in bowl and add to soup mixture.

- Bring to a boil, reduce heat and simmer for about 2 hours; stir occasionally. Serves 6 to 8.

Hearty Bean and Ham Soup

¼ cup (½ stick) butter
1 (15 ounce) can sliced carrots, drained
1 cup chopped celery
1 cup chopped green bell pepper
2 - 3 cups cooked, diced ham
2 (15 ounce) cans navy beans
2 (15 ounce) cans pinto beans
2 (14 ounce) cans chicken broth
2 teaspoons chili powder

- Combine butter, carrots, celery and bell pepper in soup pot and cook for about 8 minutes until tender-crisp.

- Add ham, beans, broth, chili powder and a little salt and pepper.

- Bring to a boil, stirring constantly, for 3 minutes. Reduce heat and simmer for 15 minutes. Serves 6 to 8.

TIP: *One (15 ounce) can jalapeno pinto beans instead of regular pinto beans gives this recipe a little get-up-and-go.*

Meat and Potato Stew

2 pounds beef stew meat
2 (15 ounce) cans new potatoes, drained
1 (15 ounce) can sliced carrots, drained
2 (10 ounce) cans French onion soup

- Season meat with a little salt and pepper and cook with 2 cups water in large pot for 1 hour.

- Add potatoes, carrots and onion soup and mix well.

- Bring to a boil, reduce heat and simmer for 30 minutes. Serves 6 to 8.

Corn Chowder

1 (14 ounce) can chicken broth
1 cup milk
1 (10 ounce) can cream of celery soup
1 (15 ounce) can cream-style corn
1 (15 ounce) can whole kernel corn
½ cup dry potato flakes
1 onion, chopped
2 - 3 cups cooked, chopped ham

- Combine all ingredients in sprayed 6-quart slow cooker.

- Cover and cook on LOW for 4 to 5 hours.

- When ready to serve, season with a little salt and pepper. Serves 6.

Country Chicken Chowder

1½ pounds boneless, skinless chicken breast halves
2 tablespoons butter
2 (10 ounce) cans cream of potato soup
1 (14 ounce) can chicken broth
1 (10 ounce) package frozen whole kernel corn
1 onion, sliced
2 ribs celery, sliced
1 (10 ounce) package frozen peas and carrots, thawed
½ teaspoon dried thyme
½ cup half-and-half cream

- Cut chicken into 1-inch strips.

- Brown chicken strips in butter in skillet and transfer to large slow cooker.

- Add soup, broth, corn, onion, celery, peas and carrots, and thyme and stir.

- Cover and cook on LOW for 3 to 4 hours or until vegetables are tender.

- Turn off heat, stir in half-and-half cream and set aside for about 10 minutes before serving. Serves 6.

Ham-Vegetable Chowder

This is a great recipe for leftover ham.

1 medium potato, peeled
2 (10 ounce) cans cream of celery soup
1 (14 ounce) can chicken broth
2 cups cooked, finely diced ham
1 (15 ounce) can whole kernel corn
2 carrots, sliced
1 onion, coarsely chopped
1 teaspoon dried basil
1 (10 ounce) package frozen broccoli florets

- Cut potato into 1-inch pieces.

- Combine all ingredients except broccoli florets in large slow cooker.

- Cover and cook on LOW for 5 to 6 hours. Add broccoli and about ½ teaspoon each of salt and pepper and cook for additional 1 hour. Serves 4.

Yummy Soup Dumplings

2 eggs, separated
Milk
2 tablespoons butter
1 cup flour

- Pour egg whites into 1-cup measure and fill with milk.

- Melt butter in cast-iron skillet or heavy pan; add flour and a pinch of salt and stir well.

- Add egg whites and milk and cook over low heat until mixture turns loose from pan. Add egg yolks and mix well.

- Drop spoonfuls of mixture into hot soup or stew and cook over medium heat, uncovered, for 10 minutes. Remove pan from heat and cover. Let stand for 10 more minutes before serving.

Legacy Potato Dumplings

4 russet potatoes
1 cup flour
1 egg, slightly beaten
1 teaspoon dry minced onion
½ cup buttered croutons
¼ cup (½ stick) butter, melted
2 tablespoons breadcrumbs
1 teaspoon shredded parmesan cheese

- Boil potatoes in large saucepan in enough water to cover until just tender, drain and cool in refrigerator overnight. Peel and shred potatoes in large bowl.

- Add flour, egg, minced onion, 2 teaspoons salt and ½ teaspoon pepper and toss gently, but thoroughly. Roll into balls about the size of medium egg. (If mixture does not stick together, add several additional tablespoons of flour and mix again.)

- Press balls flat in hands and add several croutons to mixture. Roll into ball again, carefully drop into boiling water and cook for about 8 minutes.

- Remove with slotted spoon, drain and place on platter. Pour butter over top and sprinkle with breadcrumbs mixed with parmesan cheese. Serves 4.

Old-Fashioned Butter Dumplings

¼ cup (½ stick) butter, softened
1 egg yolk
3 tablespoons flour

- Cream butter with egg yolk in bowl and beat well. Add flour a little at a time while mixing constantly.

- Drop small balls of dough into hot soup and cook for 10 minutes over high heat. Serve immediately.

TIP: This is great in soups with lots of broth without noodles or rice.

Purple Lady Salad

1 (6 ounce) package grape gelatin
1 (20 ounce) can blueberry pie filling
1 (20 ounce) can crushed pineapple
1 cup miniature marshmallows
1 cup chopped pecans

- Pour 1 cup boiling water over gelatin in large bowl and mix well.

- Add blueberry pie filling and pineapple. Refrigerate until gelatin begins to thicken. Stir in marshmallows and pecans.

- Pour into 9 x 13-inch glass dish and refrigerate. Serves 12.

TIP: *To make a completely different salad, you can fold in an 1 (8 ounce) carton whipped topping (thawed) when mixture begins to congeal.*

Divinity Salad

1 (6 ounce) package lemon gelatin
1 (8 ounce) package cream cheese, softened
¾ cup chopped pecans
1 (15 ounce) can crushed pineapple
1 (8 ounce) carton whipped topping, thawed

- Blend gelatin with 1 cup boiling water in bowl until it dissolves.

- Add cream cheese, beat slowly and increase speed until smooth. Add pecans and pineapple and refrigerate until nearly set.

- Fold in whipped topping. Pour into 9 x 13-inch dish and refrigerate. Serves 12.

The top five counties in agricultural sales in Pennsylvania are Lancaster, Chester, Berks, Franklin and Lebanon Counties.

Chilled Ambrosia Salad

This is really a make-ahead ambrosia salad.

2 (1 ounce) packages unflavored gelatin
1 (20 ounce) can crushed pineapple
⅔ cup sugar
3 tablespoons lemon juice
1 (8 ounce) package cream cheese, softened
2 (11 ounce) cans mandarin oranges, drained
⅔ cup chopped pecans
½ cup flaked coconut

- Mix gelatin with ½ cup cold water in bowl.

- Drain pineapple and add enough water to juice to make 1 cup.

- Place juice in saucepan and heat to a boil. Add gelatin mixture and stir until gelatin dissolves.

- Remove from heat, stir in sugar, lemon juice and cream cheese and blend with whisk.

- Refrigerate until mixture is consistency of egg whites (1 hour in refrigerator, but stir several times to check).

- Fold in pineapple, oranges, pecans and coconut and spoon into a 9 x 13-inch pan. Refrigerate. Serves 8.

Cranberry-Apple Salad

2 cups apple cider
2 (3 ounce) packages cranberry-raspberry gelatin
1 (15 ounce) can crushed pineapple
1 (15 ounce) whole cranberry sauce
1 cup chopped apple with peel
¼ cup chopped walnuts

- Heat apple cider and stir in gelatin until it dissolves.

- Stir in pineapple and cranberry sauce until it blends well. Cool to room temperature.

- Stir in apple and walnuts. Refrigerate until firm. Serves 8 to 10.

Marinated Beets

(Rote Rubensalat)

1½ pounds beets
1 tablespoon horseradish
2 teaspoons caraway seeds
½ cup wine vinegar
1 tablespoon sugar

- Cook beets in saucepan over medium-high heat for 30 minutes or until they are tender. Rinse in cold water and remove skins.

- Cut into very thin slices and place in large shallow dish. Sprinkle horseradish and caraway seeds over slices.

- Cook vinegar, sugar and ½ teaspoon salt in saucepan until sugar dissolves.

- Pour over beets and marinate in refrigerator for at least 2 days. Serves 6.

Broccoli-Cauliflower Salad

1 small head cauliflower
3 stalks broccoli
1 cup mayonnaise
1 tablespoon vinegar
1 tablespoon sugar
1 bunch green onions with tops, chopped
8 ounces mozzarella cheese, cubed

- Cut cauliflower and broccoli into bite-size florets and place in bowl.

- In separate bowl, combine mayonnaise, vinegar and sugar.

- Combine cauliflower, broccoli, mayonnaise mixture, onions and cheese. (Add a little salt, if you like.)

- Toss and refrigerate. Serves 10.

Best Cabbage Salad

½ pound (8 ounces) bacon
1 large onion, diced
1 medium head cabbage, coarsely chopped
4 medium tomatoes, quartered
1 green or yellow bell pepper, seeded, diced
1 tablespoon soy sauce

- Fry bacon in large skillet; drain on paper towels. Saute onion in bacon drippings until translucent.

- Combine onion, cabbage, tomatoes, bell pepper, and a little salt and pepper in large heavy pot with several inches of water.

- Cook on medium-low heat for about 15 to 20 minutes or until tender-crisp; drain.

- Add soy sauce and crumbled bacon and mix well. Serve hot or cold and store in refrigerator. Serves 8.

Home-Style Slaw

1 medium head green cabbage, shredded
½ onion, chopped
⅓ cup sugar
1 cup mayonnaise
¼ cup vinegar

- Toss cabbage and onion in bowl. Season with salt, pepper and sugar. In separate bowl, combine mayonnaise and vinegar. Pour over cabbage and onion, toss and refrigerate. Serves 6.

Marinated Cucumbers

⅓ cup vinegar
2 tablespoons sugar
1 teaspoon dried dill weed
3 cucumbers, peeled, sliced

- Combine vinegar, sugar, dill weed, 1 teaspoon salt and ¼ teaspoon pepper. Pour over cucumbers. Refrigerate 1 hour before serving. Serves 6.

Garlic Green Bean Salad

3 (15 ounce) cans whole green beans, drained
⅔ cup olive oil
½ cup vinegar
½ cup sugar
5 cloves garlic, minced
Cayenne pepper

- Place green beans in container with lid. Mix oil, vinegar, sugar and garlic in bowl and pour over beans. Sprinkle with a little salt and cayenne pepper. Refrigerate overnight. Serves 8 to 10.

Winter Bean Medley

1 (15 ounce) can French-style green beans, drained
1 (15 ounce) can black-eyed peas, drained
1 (15 ounce) can whole kernal corn, drained
1 (16 ounce) can green peas, drained
1 (2 ounce) jar diced pimentos, drained
1 bell pepper, chopped
1 onion, sliced, broken into rings

- Be sure to drain vegetables well before combining.

- Combine all salad ingredients in 3-quart container with lid and gently mix.

Dressing:

¾ cup sugar
1 teaspoon seasoned salt
½ teaspoon garlic powder
½ cup olive oil
¾ cup vinegar

- Combine sugar, seasoned salt, garlic powder, olive oil, vinegar, and 1 teaspoon each of salt and pepper.

- Pour over vegetables and stir. Cover and refrigerate. Serves 16.

TIP: *Keep a supply of these ingredients on hand because when you need to take a dish to a friend, it's a salad in a hurry.*

Chilled Baby Lima Bean Salad

2 (10 ounce) packages frozen baby lima beans
1 (15 ounce) can whole kernal corn, drained
1 bunch green onions with tops, chopped
1 cup mayonnaise
2 teaspoons ranch salad dressing seasoning

- Cook beans according to package directions and drain.

- Add corn, onions, mayonnaise and seasoning; mix well and refrigerate. Serves 8.

German Potato Salad

4 medium Irish potatoes
12 slices bacon
¼ cup tarragon vinegar
½ cup chopped onions
2 tablespoons chopped green bell pepper
¼ cup pickle relish
2 tablespoons capers
1 teaspoon celery salt
2 eggs, hard-boiled, thinly sliced

- Boil potatoes until tender and set aside to cool.

- Fry bacon in skillet until crisp and drain; set aside drippings. When cool break into small pieces and set aside.

- Pour vinegar and several tablespoons warm water into hot bacon drippings, mix well and remove from heat.

- Peel potatoes, cube and place in large bowl. Add onions, bell pepper, relish, capers and celery salt.

- Pour vinegar-bacon drippings over potatoes and carefully toss. Set aside at room temperature for several hours and stir occasionally.

- Place slices of egg on top and serve. Garnish with bacon pieces. Serves 4.

Hot German Potato Salad

2½ pounds boiling potatoes
8 slices bacon
1 tablespoon flour
½ cup vinegar
1 teaspoon sugar
1 cup chopped green onions with tops
2 teaspoons chopped fresh parsley

- Wash potatoes and remove bad spots. Boil potatoes in enough water to cover in large pot until tender. Use 1 teaspoon salt for each quart water in pot.

- When cool, peel and dice potatoes and place in large bowl.

- Fry bacon in skillet until crisp, drain on paper towel and crumble when cool.

- Add flour to bacon drippings and cook over medium heat, stirring constantly.

- Slowly pour in ½ cup water while stirring, increase heat and cook until drippings boil and thicken.

- Add vinegar, sugar, onions and 2 teaspoons salt to bacon dressing and mix well.

- Pour hot dressing over potatoes, gently toss and sprinkle with parsley. Serve immediately. Serves 4 to 6.

Groundhog Day (February 2) is celebrated in Punxsutawney, Pennsylvania where a local groundhog named Punxsutawney Phil makes his famous weather prediction of whether there will be six more weeks of winter. This tradition dates back to the early German settlers in Pennsylvania and harks back to a custom that hedgehogs could predict how much winter was left. But hedgehogs are not native to North America, so pioneers looked at groundhogs instead.

Sweet Potato Salad

4 medium sweet potatoes
8 slices bacon
½ cup minced onion
Canola oil
Sugar
Vinegar

- Boil sweet potatoes in saucepan until tender and drain. When cool peel potatoes and cube. Place cubed potatoes in large bowl.

- Fry bacon in skillet until crisp. Drain, cool and crumble.

- Add a little oil to bacon drippings, add onion and cook over low heat for several minutes.

- Cool slightly and add sugar and vinegar to taste.

- Pour dressing over sweet potatoes and gently toss.

- Let stand at room temperature for about 15 minutes. Stir again and sprinkle bacon over top. Serves 5 to 6.

Special Spinach Salad

1 (10 ounce) package fresh spinach
1 (15 ounce) can bean sprouts, drained
8 slices bacon, cooked crisp
1 (8 ounce) can water chestnuts, chopped
Vinaigrette salad dressing

- Combine spinach and bean sprouts in bowl.

- When ready to serve, add crumbled bacon and water chestnuts.

- Toss with vinaigrette salad dressing (or make your own with 3 parts olive oil and 1 part red wine vinegar). Serves 4.

Spring Greens Salad

1 (5 ounce) package fresh spring greens salad mix
¾ cup quartered strawberries, drained
⅓ cup pistachios, coarsely chopped
⅓ cup raisins
1 large ripe avocado
Lemon juice
⅓ cup blue cheese crumbles
Raspberry dressing

- Toss spring greens, strawberries, pistachios and raisins in bowl gently and refrigerate.

- Just before serving, peel and slice avocado. Sprinkle a little lemon juice over slices. Sprinkle blue cheese crumbles and avocado on top of salad. Serve dressing on the side. Serves 4.

Cornbread Salad Surprise

2 (6 ounce) packages Mexican cornbread mix
2 eggs
1⅓ cup milk
2 ribs celery, sliced
1 bunch green onions with tops, chopped
1 green bell pepper, chopped
2 tomatoes, chopped, drained
8 slices bacon, cooked, crumbled
1 cup shredded cheddar cheese
1 (8 ounce) can whole kernel corn, drained
½ cup ripe olives, chopped
2½ cups mayonnaise

- Prepare cornbread with eggs and milk according to package directions. Cook, cool and crumble cornbread in large bowl.

- Add celery, green onions, bell pepper, tomatoes, bacon, cheese, corn, olives and mayonnaise and mix well. Serves 16.

Chicken Waldorf Salad

1 pound boneless, skinless chicken breasts
1 red apple with peel, sliced
1 green apple with peel, sliced
1 cup sliced celery
½ cup chopped walnuts
2 (6 ounce) cartons orange yogurt
½ cup mayonnaise
1 (6 ounce) package shredded lettuce

- Place chicken in large saucepan and cover with water. Cook on high heat for about 15 minutes. Drain and cool.

- Cut into 1-inch chunks and season with a little salt and pepper and place in large bowl.

- Add apples, celery and walnuts. Stir in yogurt and mayonnaise. Toss to mix well.

- Serve over shredded lettuce. (May be served at room temperature or refrigerated for several hours). Serves 4 to 6.

Apple-Cranberry Green Salad

1 (10 ounce) packaged mixed salad greens
2 apples, sliced
½ cup walnut halves
1 cup Craisins®
½ cup sliced green onions
¾ cup raspberry vinaigrette

- Toss all ingredients except dressing in large bowl. Add dressing and mix. Serve immediately or refrigerate before serving. Serves 10.

More than 93% of farms in Pennsylvania are individually or family owned.

Philly Cheese Steak

This is one of Philadelphia's claims to fame and a visit to the city is not complete without eating a Philly Cheese Steak sandwich.

Canola oil
1 bell pepper, sliced
1 onion, sliced
8 mushrooms, sliced
1 tomato, seeded, sliced
16 very thin slices premium cooked roast beef or round steak
4 slices American cheese
4 premium Italian rolls
Pizza sauce, optional
Pickles, optional
Sweet or hot peppers, optional

- With hot oil in large skillet, saute bell pepper, onion and mushrooms until onion is translucent.

- Add tomato and slices of beef and cook just long enough to get beef hot. Remove from heat.

- Place cheese into Italian roll and place vegetables and beef on top.

- Spread pizza sauce, pickles and/or sweet or hot peppers on top and eat immediately. Serves 4.

The Big Mac was invented by Jim Delligatti in Uniontown, Pennsylvania. In 1968, McDonald's added it to their menu across the country.

The Reuben Sandwich

Butter
2 slices rye bread
1 slice Swiss cheese
Generous slices corned beef
2 tablespoons or more sauerkraut
Thousand island dressing

- Butter 1 slice bread on 1 side. Place butter-side down in skillet over low heat.

- Layer cheese, corned beef and sauerkraut on bread and spread dressing on 1 side of other slice.

- Butter opposite side of slice. Place butter-side up on sauerkraut.

- Cook until bottom browns, turn carefully and brown other side. Serves 1.

Bratwurst Heroes

1 (6 - 8 count) package cooked bratwurst sausages
Hot dog buns
1 cup refrigerated marinara sauce
1 (8 ounce) jar roasted bell peppers
6 - 8 slices pepper-Jack cheese

- Heat bratwurst on grill until hot and turn frequently. When brats are just about done, toast buns cut side down on grill.

- Heat marinara sauce in saucepan and place brats on toasted buns.

- Layer bell peppers, marinara sauce and cheese over bratwurst. Serves 6 to 8.

The Lancaster County area attracts more than 5 million visitors each year. The original settlers were mostly German (Deutsch) and became known as "Pennsylvania Dutch".

Corned Beef Open-Face Sandwiches

8 slices rye bread
Mustard
16 ounces thinly sliced corned or roast beef
8 slices cheddar cheese

Mustard Dressing:

¾ cup mayonnaise
1 tablespoon mustard
2 teaspoons horseradish, optional
½ teaspoon Worcestershire sauce
1 teaspoon sweet pickle relish
Dash hot sauce, optional

- Preheat broiler.

- Spread bread slices with prepared mustard and place on foil-lined baking sheet, mustard side up. Top with corned beef, then cheese.

- Mix all ingredients for dressing until they blend well.

- Spread each open-face sandwich with mustard dressing to within ½-inch of edge. Place under broiler until cheese melts and dressing bubbles. Serves 8.

Henry J. Heinz (1844-1919) was born in Pittsburgh, Pennsylvania. His family moved to Sharpsburg, Pennsylvania when he was 5. By the age of 8, he was going from door to door selling vegetables from the family garden and was growing, manufacturing and selling his own brand of horseradish sauce by age 9. One of Heinz's first products was tomato ketchup. In 1888, he bought out his partners and founded the H.J. Heinz Company. He launched the company's famous slogan, "57 varieties", in 1896.

Vegetables and Side Dishes

State Flag

The flag of Pennsylvania is a blue field (same blue as that of the U.S. flag) on which the state's coat of arms is embroidered or printed. The coat of arms consists of a shield on which symbols of a ship, a plough and sheaves of wheat appear. An eagle is at the top of the shield and a stalk of corn and an olive branch cross at the bottom. Two draft horses support the sides and the motto, "Virtue, Liberty and Independence", appears on a banner below.

Easy Parmesan Broccoli

1 (16 ounce) package frozen broccoli spears
½ teaspoon garlic powder
½ cup breadcrumbs
¼ cup (½ stick) butter, melted
½ cup grated parmesan cheese

- Cook broccoli in saucepan according to package directions.

- Drain and add garlic powder, breadcrumbs, butter and cheese. Add salt, if you like, and toss.

- Heat and serve. Serves 6.

Marinated Brussels Sprouts

2 (10 ounce) boxes frozen brussels sprouts
1 cup Italian dressing
1 cup chopped red bell pepper
½ cup chopped onion

- Pierce boxes of brussels sprouts and microwave for 7 minutes.

- Mix Italian dressing, bell pepper and onion in bowl.

- Pour over brussels sprouts and marinate for at least 24 hours. Drain to serve. Serves 6 to 8.

The York Fair is the oldest agricultural fair in the country. In 1765, York was granted the privilege of holding two fairs each year in the spring and the fall. While there was a hiatus in fairs after 1815, the York Fair was reinstituted in 1853 and has been held every year since.

Favorite Sweet-and-Sour Cabbage

2 slices bacon
1 medium head cabbage, chopped
2 green bell peppers, seeded, chopped
2 medium onions, chopped
1 cup vinegar
¼ cup sugar

- Fry bacon in skillet until crisp, drain and set aside drippings and bacon.

- Place cabbage, bell peppers and onions in large saucepan.

- Pour vinegar, sugar and 3 cups water into small saucepan. Cook over medium heat and stir until sugar dissolves. Pour mixture over cabbage and cook for about 15 minutes or until cabbage is just tender and changes color.

- Sprinkle with a little salt and pepper. Crumble bacon over top and pour in bacon drippings. Mix well. Serve immediately or store in refrigerator and serve cold or heated. It's better after it is stored for awhile. Serves 6.

Easy Red Cabbage

1 head red cabbage, sliced
2 tablespoons butter
1 tablespoon minced onion
¼ teaspoon cayenne pepper
2 tablespoons vinegar
1 tablespoon sugar

- Soak cabbage in cold water for 30 to 45 minutes. Drain and place in large saucepan.

- Add butter, onion, cayenne pepper and a little salt. Add enough water to barely cover and cook over medium-high heat until just tender.

- Add vinegar and sugar and cook for additional 5 minutes. Serve immediately. Serves 4.

Easy Baked Cabbage

1 large head cabbage, chopped
3 tablespoons butter
1 (2 ounce) jar diced pimentos, drained well
1 egg
1 cup milk
1 cup crushed cornflakes

- Preheat oven to 350°.

- Place cabbage in enough boiling water to cover and cook until tender. Season with a little salt and pepper. Remove from heat and drain well. Add butter and pimentos and stir well until butter melts.

- Pour cabbage into sprayed 7 x 11-inch baking dish. Mix egg, milk and cornflakes in bowl and pour over cabbage. Bake until firm. Serve 4 to 5.

Family-Meal Cooked Sauerkraut

This is a lot better if you make it the day before you serve it.

2 quarts canned sauerkraut
4 slices bacon
1 large onion, minced
2 medium apples, peeled, cored, chopped
1 tablespoon caraway seeds
1 large potato

- Drain sauerkraut in strainer, press out all liquid and set aside. Fry bacon in skillet over high heat and drain.

- Add onion, apples, caraway seeds and sauerkraut to skillet. Crumble bacon over mixture and stir well. Add about half enough water to cover and cook, covered, over medium heat for about 2 hours. Add water if needed.

- Peel and grate potato and add to skillet. Cook for additional 20 minutes to thicken. Serves 6 to 8.

Brown Sugar Carrots

1 (16 ounce) package baby carrots
¾ cup orange juice
2 tablespoons butter
2 tablespoons brown sugar
½ teaspoon ground cumin

- Combine all ingredients and ¼ cup water in saucepan.

- Cook on medium-high for about 10 minutes or until carrots are tender and liquid cooks out. Serves 6.

Creamed Carrots

¼ cup (½ stick) butter
3 tablespoons flour
1½ cups milk
2 (15 ounce) cans sliced carrots

- Melt butter in saucepan and add flour plus ½ teaspoon salt and mix well.

- Cook milk with butter-flour mixture over medium heat and stir constantly. Cook until mixture thickens.

- In smaller saucepan, heat carrots and drain. Add carrots to milk mixture and serve hot. Serves 6 to 8.

Crunchy Sauteed Celery

1 bunch celery, chopped diagonally
1 (8 ounce) can water chestnuts, drained, chopped
¼ cup almonds, toasted
¼ cup (½ stick) butter, melted

- Boil celery in salted water in saucepan just until tender-crisp and drain.

- Saute water chestnuts and almonds in melted butter in skillet.

- Toss celery and water chestnuts-almond mixture. Serve hot. Serves 4.

Super Corn Casserole

1 (15 ounce) can whole kernel corn
1 (15 ounce) can cream-style corn
½ cup (1 stick) butter, melted
1 (8 ounce) carton sour cream
1 (6 ounce) package cornbread mix

- Preheat oven to 350°.

- Mix all ingredients in bowl and pour into sprayed 9 x 13-inch baking dish.

- Bake uncovered for 35 minutes. Serves 8 to 10.

TIP: *To add a little zip to this recipe, use 1 (6 ounce) package jalapeno cornbread mix instead of plain cornbread mix.*

Festive Shoe-Peg Corn

1 (8 ounce) package cream cheese, softened
½ cup (1 stick) butter, softened
3 (15 ounce) cans shoe-peg or white corn

- Preheat oven to 350°.

- Beat cream cheese and butter in bowl. Add corn and mix well. Spoon into sprayed 9 x 13-inch baking dish.

- Cover and bake for 30 minutes. Serves 12.

Short-Cut Corn Pudding

1 (8 ounce) package corn muffin mix
1 (15 ounce) can cream-style corn
½ cup sour cream
3 eggs, slightly beaten

- Preheat oven to 350°.

- Combine all ingredients in bowl and pour in sprayed 2-quart baking dish.

- Bake uncovered for about 35 minutes. Serves 4 to 6.

Green Beans with Mushrooms

½ cup (1 stick) butter, divided
1 small onion, chopped
1 (8 ounce) carton fresh mushrooms, sliced
2 pounds fresh green beans, trimmed
¾ cup chicken broth

- Melt ¼ cup butter in saucepan, saute onion and mushrooms and transfer to small bowl.

- In same saucepan, melt remaining butter and toss with green beans.

- Pour chicken broth over beans and bring to a boil. Reduce heat, cover and simmer until liquid evaporates and green beans are tender-crisp.

- Stir in mushroom mixture and season with a little salt and pepper. Serves 8.

Nutty Green Beans

1 (16 ounce) package frozen green beans, thawed
¼ cup (½ stick) butter
¾ cup pine nuts
½ teaspoon garlic powder
½ teaspoon celery salt

- Cook beans in ½ cup water in 3-quart saucepan, covered, for 10 to 15 minutes or until beans are tender-crisp and drain.

- Melt butter in skillet over medium heat and add pine nuts. Cook, stirring frequently, until golden.

- Add pine nuts to green beans and season with garlic powder, celery salt, ½ teaspoon salt and ½ teaspoon pepper. Serves 6.

Pennsylvania accounts for 61% of total U.S. mushroom sales with California a distant second with 14%.

Creamy Limas

2 (16 ounce) packages frozen lima beans, thawed
2 tablespoons butter
½ teaspoon sugar
1 cup half-and-half cream

- Place lima beans, butter, sugar, ½ cup water and a little salt and pepper in large saucepan.

- Bring to a boil, reduce heat to medium, cover and cook for 10 minutes or until water evaporates.

- Pour half-and-half cream over mixture, increase heat to high and cook almost to boiling.

- Remove from heat and cover. Let stand for about 5 to 10 minutes for cream to thicken. Serves 4.

Better Butter Beans

1 cup sliced celery
1 onion, chopped
¼ cup (½ stick) butter
1 (10 ounce) can diced tomatoes and green chilies
½ teaspoon sugar
2 (15 ounce) cans butter beans

- Saute celery and onion in butter in skillet for about 3 minutes.

- Add tomatoes and green chilies, several sprinkles of salt, and sugar.

- Add butter beans, cover and simmer for about 20 minutes. Serve hot. Serves 8.

Bowers, Pennsylvania claims to host the largest chile pepper festival in the country with 10,000 people attending each year. There is a jalapeno-eating contest at this two-day event held in early fall and lots of red-hot chile peppers to take home.

Buttery Baked Onions

4 large sweet onions
½ cup (1 stick) butter

- Preheat oven to 350°.

- Hollow out cavity in center of onions, but do not cut through to other side.

- Place 2 tablespoons butter in each onion. Sprinkle with a little salt and a lot of pepper.

- Place in sprayed baking dish and bake for 30 to 45 minutes or until onions are tender. Serves 4.

Creamed Spinach Bake

2 (10 ounce) packages frozen chopped spinach
2 (3 ounce) packages cream cheese, softened
3 tablespoons butter
1 cup seasoned breadcrumbs

- Preheat oven to 350°.

- Cook spinach in saucepan according to package directions and drain.

- Combine cream cheese and butter with spinach. Heat until cream cheese and butter melt and mix well with spinach.

- Pour into sprayed baking dish and sprinkle a little salt over spinach.

- Cover with breadcrumbs and bake for 15 to 20 minutes. Serves 8.

Mushrooms help build resistance to colds because they contain ergothioneine, an antioxidant that boosts the immune system, according to a study by Pennsylvania State University.

Toasted Spinach with Pine Nuts

1 (16 ounce) package frozen leaf spinach, thawed
¼ cup (½ stick) butter
2 cloves garlic, finely minced
5 green onions with tops, chopped
½ teaspoon seasoned salt
¼ teaspoon celery salt
½ cup pine nuts

- Preheat broiler.

- Cook spinach according to package directions. Drain thoroughly. Melt butter in saucepan and add garlic, green onions, seasoned salt and celery salt. Mix well, pour over spinach and toss.

- Place in sprayed 2-quart baking dish and sprinkle pine nuts over top. Place under broiler, brown nuts slightly and serve hot. Serves 6.

Spinach-Stuffed Shells

1 (12 ounce) package jumbo pasta shells
2 (9 ounce) packages frozen creamed spinach
1 (15 ounce) carton ricotta cheese
1 (8 ounce) package shredded mozzarella cheese
½ pound ground beef
1 (26 ounce) jar spaghetti sauce

- Preheat oven to 350°.

- Prepare pasta according to package directions. Drain.

- Prepare spinach according to package directions and cool slightly. Add ricotta, mozzarella and 1 teaspoon salt to spinach. Stuff each shell with 1 tablespoon mixture.

- Cook meat in skillet and add spaghetti sauce. Place shells in sprayed 9 x 13-inch baking dish and pour sauce over all. Bake for 30 minutes. Serves 6 to 8.

Farmer's White Squash Pudding

2 white squash, peeled, cubed
¾ cup sugar, divided
1 tablespoon cornstarch
1½ cups milk
2 eggs, separated
½ teaspoon lemon extract

- Preheat oven to 325°.

- Boil squash in just enough salted water to cover in saucepan until tender.

- Drain and place in sprayed 7 x 11-inch baking dish.

- In small bowl, mix ½ cup sugar, cornstarch and milk and stir until well blended.

- Add egg yolks and lemon extract and pour over squash. Bake about 20 minutes or until mixture is firm.

- Just before squash is done, beat egg whites in bowl until stiff. Add ¼ cup sugar and beat until stiff peaks form.

- Spread over squash and return to oven until egg whites are slightly brown on top. Serves 4 to 6.

Fried Yellow Squash or Zucchini

2 large yellow squash or zucchini, sliced
1 egg, beaten
2 tablespoons milk
¾ cup cornmeal
¾ cup flour
Canola oil

- Place squash on plate and sprinkle with a little salt and pepper. Combine egg and milk in bowl.

- In separate shallow bowl, combine cornmeal and flour.

- Dip squash slices in egg-milk mixture and then in cornmeal-flour mixture. Fry in skillet in a little hot oil. Drain on paper towel. Serves 4 to 6.

Sunny Yellow Squash

2 pounds small-medium yellow squash, sliced
2 onions, coarsely chopped
3 ribs celery, diagonally sliced
1 red bell pepper, seeded, julienned
1 green bell pepper, seeded, julienned
1 (8 ounce) package cream cheese, cubed
½ teaspoon sugar
¼ cup (½ stick) butter, melted
1 (10 ounce) can fiesta nacho cheese soup
1½ cups seasoned croutons

- Preheat oven to 350°.

- Combine squash, onions, celery and bell peppers in large saucepan.

- Add about 1 cup water and cook for about 10 minutes or until tender-crisp. Drain well.

- While still hot, stir in cream cheese, sugar, 1 teaspoon salt, 1 teaspoon pepper, butter and soup and stir just enough for cream cheese to melt and blend.

- Pour into sprayed 9 x 13-inch baking dish. Sprinkle croutons on top and bake for about 20 minutes. Serves 8.

TIP: If you don't want black specks in this dish, use white pepper.

Buttery Squash and Onion

8 yellow squash, sliced
2 onions, chopped
¼ cup (½ stick) butter, melted
1 cup shredded American cheese

- Cook squash and onions in small amount of water in saucepan until tender and drain.

- Add butter and cheese, toss and serve hot. Serves 6 to 8.

Cream-Style Zucchini

5 large zucchini, sliced
½ onion, chopped
1 (15 ounce) can cream-style corn
1 (8 ounce) package cream cheese, softened
1 tablespoon cornstarch
1 (4 ounce) can diced green chilies, drained
1½ cups cracker crumbs

- Preheat oven to 350°.

- Cook zucchini and onion in boiling water in saucepan just until tender-crisp and drain well.

- Add corn, cream cheese and cornstarch, leave on low burner and stir until cream cheese melts.

- Stir in green chilies, 1 teaspoon salt and ½ teaspoon pepper.

- Pour in sprayed 9 x 13-inch baking dish and top with cracker crumbs.

- Bake for 45 minutes. Serves 8 to 10.

Baked Tomatoes

2 (15 ounce) cans diced tomatoes, drained
1½ cups breadcrumbs, divided
Scant ¼ cup sugar
½ onion, chopped
¼ cup (½ stick) butter, melted

- Preheat oven to 325º.

- Combine tomatoes, 1 cup breadcrumbs, sugar, ½ teaspoon salt, onion and butter.

- Pour into 2-quart sprayed baking dish and cover with remaining breadcrumbs.

- Bake uncovered for 20 to 25 minutes or until crumbs are light brown. Serves 8.

Old-Fashioned Scraped New Potatoes

8 small new potatoes, scrubbed clean
2 tablespoons breadcrumbs, toasted

- Place potatoes in large bowl of water (dipping potato in water as you scrape off skin speeds up scraping time).

- Scrape toward you with paring knife, holding potato firmly in one hand and guiding knife with other. Do not pare, but scrape gently, with blade at 90° angle to potato, until all skin is removed.

- Place scraped potatoes in separate bowl filled with cold water to prevent them from turning brown.

- When ready to cook, place potatoes in large saucepan with 2 cups water and ½ teaspoon salt and cook over medium heat with lid cracked until tender, about 20 minutes. Edges should crack; if they don't, just prick potato with fork several times.

- Drain and place in heated serving dish. Top with toasted breadcrumbs. Serves 4.

TIP: Don't bother trying to scrape new potatoes for a large dinner party if you haven't tried it before. It takes about 1 hour to scrape enough for 6 people. Of course, it is well worth the effort, but I would suggest preparing them the day before and storing them in cold water until needed. When you buy new potatoes, scrape one with your nail. If the skin does not come off easily, they are not freshly dug and will be hard to scrape.

The Troy Fair has been held annually for over 130 years. This week-long event includes food preparation contests, shows and entertainment and the traditional crop and livestock competitions. It's usually held in July in Troy, Pennsylvania and attracts more than 100,000 visitors.

Colorful Roasted Potatoes

18 - 20 small, new (red) potatoes with peels
½ cup (1 stick) butter, melted
2 (4 ounce) cans diced green chilies
2 tablespoons fresh snipped parsley
½ teaspoon garlic powder
½ teaspoon paprika

- Steam potatoes in large saucepan with small amount of water until tender. (Test with fork.)

- In separate saucepan, combine butter, green chilies, parsley, garlic powder, 1 teaspoon salt and ½ teaspoon pepper. Heat until ingredients mix well.

- Place potatoes in serving dish, spoon butter mixture over potatoes and sprinkle with paprika. Serves 6 to 8.

Dinner-Bell Mashed Potatoes

8 medium to large potatoes
1 (8 ounce) carton sour cream
1 (8 ounce) package cream cheese, softened
Butter

- Preheat oven to 325°.

- Peel, cut up and boil potatoes in saucepan until tender and drain.

- Whip hot potatoes and add sour cream, cream cheese, 1 teaspoon salt and ½ teaspoon pepper. Continue whipping until cream cheese melts.

- Pour in sprayed 3-quart baking dish. Dot generously with butter.

- Cover and bake for about 20 minutes. Serves 8 to 10.

Cheesy Good Potatoes

6 medium potatoes
½ cup (1 stick) butter, sliced
1 tablespoon flour
1 (16 ounce) package shredded cheddar cheese
¾ cup milk

- Preheat oven to 350°.

- Peel and wash potatoes, slice half the potatoes and place in sprayed 3-quart baking dish.

- Arrange half the butter over potatoes and sprinkle with flour. Cover with half the cheese.

- Slice remaining potatoes, place over first layer and add remaining sliced butter.

- Pour milk over casserole and sprinkle with remaining cheese.

- Cover and bake for 1 hour. Serves 8.

TIP: *This must be cooked immediately or potatoes will darken. It may be frozen after baking and reheated or made the day before and reheated.*

Favorite Potato Pancakes

3 pounds white potatoes, peeled, grated
1 onion, finely minced
3 eggs, beaten
½ cup seasoned dry breadcrumbs
Canola oil

- Combine potatoes, onions, eggs, breadcrumbs, and a little salt and pepper. Mix well.

- Drop spoonfuls of mixture in skillet in hot oil and brown on both sides. Serves 8 to 10.

German Fried Potatoes

4 medium potatoes with peels
2 slices bacon, diced
1 medium onion, chopped

- Boil potatoes in saucepan with enough water to cover; cook until tender. Drain and cut/slice to make strips the size you want.

- Fry bacon in large skillet until crisp. Remove bacon and crumble. Add potatoes and onions to drippings and fry until potatoes are golden brown.

- Before serving, sprinkle with salt and pepper and crumbled bacon. Serves 4 to 6.

Quick Potato Fritters

1 cup mashed potatoes
1 egg, beaten
⅓ cup flour
¼ cup milk
Canola oil

- Mix all ingredients except oil. Heat about ¼ inch oil in skillet.

- Shape fritter mixture into patties and drop into hot oil. When patties are brown around edges and set, turn over and brown the other side. Serves 4 to 6.

Hot Chive-Potato Souffle

3 eggs, separated
2 cups hot prepared instant mashed potatoes
½ cup sour cream
2 heaping tablespoons chopped chives

- Preheat oven to 325°.

- Beat egg whites until stiff and set aside. Beat yolks until smooth and add to potatoes.

- Fold beaten egg whites, sour cream, chives and ½ teaspoon salt into potato-egg yolk mixture and pour into sprayed 2-quart baking dish. Bake for 45 minutes. Serves 6.

The Best Sweet Potato Casserole

1 (29 ounce) can sweet potatoes, drained
⅓ cup evaporated milk
¾ cup sugar
2 eggs, beaten
¼ cup (½ stick) butter, melted
1 teaspoon vanilla

- Preheat oven to 350°.

- Place sweet potatoes in bowl and mash slightly with fork.

- Add evaporated milk, sugar, eggs, butter and vanilla and mix well.

- Pour mixture into sprayed 7 x 11-inch baking dish. Sprinkle with topping.

Topping:

1 cup packed light brown sugar
⅓ cup (⅔ stick) butter, melted
½ cup flour
1 cup chopped pecans

- Combine brown sugar, butter, flour and pecans in bowl and sprinkle over top of casserole.

- Bake uncovered for 35 minutes or until crusty on top. Serves 8.

Fried Sweet Potatoes

1½ pounds sweet potatoes
Canola oil

- Wash potatoes and place in large saucepan with about 2 to 3 cups water. Cover and cook over medium heat for about 20 minutes or until tender.

- Remove from saucepan and cool. Remove skin and cut into ½-inch slices. Heat just enough oil to cover bottom of large skillet. Place sweet potatoes in hot oil and fry until slices are brown on both sides. Drain on paper towels, salt lightly and serve hot. Serves 4.

Country Cornbread Dressing

1 (8 ounce) box cornbread mix
1 egg, beaten
⅓ cup milk
8 slices bacon
1 cup diced celery
½ cup minced onion
3 tablespoons snipped fresh parsley
1½ cups chicken broth

- Preheat oven to 350°.

- Prepare cornbread mix with egg and milk according to package directions and bake.

- When cornbread cools, crumble into small pieces.

- Fry bacon in large skillet over high heat until crispy. Drain on paper towels and crumble when cool.

- Discard all but 2 tablespoons bacon drippings and saute celery, onion and parsley in skillet until onion is translucent.

- Add broth, bacon and crumbled cornbread to skillet and mix well.

- Pour into sprayed baking dish and bake for about 35 minutes or until sides pull away from dish. Yields dressing for 1 chicken.

One of the best county fairs in Pennsylvania, the Westmoreland Fair is located near Greensburg, Pennsylvania and fills nine days with exhibits, contests, activities and entertainment. Held in midsummer, the fair features livestock exhibitors from 4H participants to farmers with competitions ranging from llamas to draft horses. Food contests and demonstrations are a part of the fair.

Cornbread Dressing and Gravy

2 (6 ounce) packages cornbread mix
9 biscuits or 1 recipe of biscuit mix
1 small onion, chopped
2 ribs celery, chopped
2 eggs
2 teaspoons poultry seasoning
3 (14 ounce) cans chicken broth, divided

- A day or two ahead of time, prepare biscuits and cornbread according to package instructions.

- Preheat oven to 350°.

- Crumble cornbread and biscuits into large bowl.

- Add onion, celery, eggs, poultry seasoning and a little pepper.

- Stir in 2½ cans chicken broth. (If the mixture is not "runny", add remaining broth. If it is still not runny, add a little milk.)

- Bake in sprayed 9 x 13-inch glass baking dish for about 45 minutes or until golden brown. (This may be frozen uncooked, thawed and cooked when you want it.)

Gravy:

2 heaping tablespoons cornstarch
2 (14 ounce) cans chicken broth, divided
2 eggs, hard-boiled, sliced

- Mix cornstarch with ½ cup broth in saucepan and mix until well blended.

- Add remaining broth and heat to boiling, stirring constantly, until broth thickens.

- Add hard-boiled eggs and a little pepper; pour into gravy boat. Serves 8 to 10.

Main Dishes

Beef
Chicken
Lamb
Pork
Seafood
Game

State Game Bird: *Ruffed Grouse*

State Mammal: *Whitetail Deer*

State Fish: *Brook Trout*

Family Cabbage Rolls

This is a wonderful family recipe and a super way to get the kids to eat cabbage. Everyone who has ever had a garden has probably made some version of these well-loved cabbage rolls.

1 large head cabbage, cored
1½ pounds lean ground beef
1 egg, beaten
3 tablespoons ketchup
⅓ cup seasoned breadcrumbs
2 tablespoons dried minced onion flakes
2 (15 ounce) cans Italian stewed tomatoes
¼ cup cornstarch
3 tablespoons brown sugar
2 tablespoons Worcestershire sauce

- Preheat oven to 325°.

- Place head of cabbage in large soup pot of boiling water for 10 minutes or until outer leaves are tender. Drain well. Rinse in cold water and remove 10 large outer leaves*. Set aside.

- Slice or shred remaining cabbage. Place in sprayed 9 x 13-inch baking dish.

- Combine ground beef, egg, ketchup, breadcrumbs, onion flakes and 1 teaspoon salt in large bowl and mix well.

- Pack together about ½ cup meat mixture and place on each cabbage leaf. Fold in sides and roll leaf to completely enclose filling. (You may have to remove thick vein from cabbage leaves for easier rolling.) Place each rolled leaf over shredded cabbage.

- Place stewed tomatoes in large saucepan. Combine cornstarch, brown sugar and Worcestershire sauce in bowl and spoon mixture into tomatoes. Cook on high heat, stirring constantly until stewed tomatoes and juices thicken. Pour over cabbage rolls. Cover and bake for 1 hour. Serves 10.

TIP: To get that many large leaves, you may have to put 2 smaller leaves together to make one roll.

Traditional Shepherd's Pie

1½ pounds ground beef
1 large onion, chopped
1 cup chopped carrots
¾ cup chopped celery
1 cup sliced mushrooms or 1 (6 ounce) can
2 tablespoons butter
½ cup frozen green peas
2 teaspoons Worcestershire sauce
½ cup beef broth
2 tablespoons flour
4 cups mashed potatoes, seasoned with salt, pepper and butter

- Preheat oven to 400°.

- Brown beef in skillet; drain fat and set aside beef.

- In same skillet, saute onion, carrots, celery and mushrooms in butter until onions are translucent.   Add peas, beef, Worcestershire sauce, broth, and salt and pepper.   Simmer for 10 minutes.   Mix flour with ¼ cup water and add to mixture; cook and stir until thick.

- Place in 9 x 13-inch baking dish.   Spread mashed potatoes on top and swirl into peaks.   Bake for 25 to 30 minutes or until potatoes are golden.   Serves 6.

A turning point of the Civil War, the Battle of Gettysburg was fought over a three-day period, July 1-3, 1863, in and around the town of Gettysburg, Pennsylvania. The citizens of Gettysburg established the "Soldiers Cemetery" for burial of the Union dead; this is now a national cemetery. The dedication on November 19, 1863, is world-famous for President Abraham Lincoln's delivery of the Gettysburg Address.

Simple Beef Stroganoff

1 pound round steak, cut into thin strips
½ cup sliced onion
1 (10 ounce) can cream of mushroom soup
½ cup sour cream
Noodles, cooked

- Brown meat and onion in skillet and drain. Add soup, sour cream and ½ cup water. Simmer for 45 minutes or until tender. Serve over noodles. Serves 4 to 6.

Simmered Pepper Steak

This is an easy way to fix steak!

½ cup flour, divided
1½ pounds round steak, cut in ½-inch strips
¼ cup canola oil
1 (15 ounce) can diced tomatoes
½ cup chopped onion
1 small clove garlic, minced
1 tablespoon beef bouillon granules
1½ teaspoons Worcestershire sauce
2 large green bell peppers, seeded, julienned
Rice, cooked

- Combine ¼ cup flour, ½ teaspoon salt and ¼ teaspoon pepper in bowl and coat steak. Heat oil in large skillet and brown meat on both sides.

- Add tomatoes, 1 cup water, onion, garlic and bouillon granules. Cover and simmer for 1 hour 15 minutes or until meat is tender.

- Uncover and add Worcestershire sauce and bell peppers. Thicken gravy with remaining flour mixed with ¼ cup cold water. Add to steak mixture. Cover and simmer for additional 5 minutes. Serve over rice. Serves 4 to 6.

Traditional Sauerbraten

1 cup dry red wine
½ cup red wine vinegar
2 bay leaves
1 teaspoon crushed black peppercorns
½ teaspoon whole cloves
¼ teaspoon ground ginger
1 (3 - 4) pound chuck roast
3 tablespoons canola oil
4 ribs celery, chopped
3 medium carrots, grated
1 onion, chopped
3 tablespoons flour

- Combine wine, vinegar, bay leaves, peppercorns, cloves, ginger and 1½ cups water in saucepan and bring to boil. Remove from heat. Place roast in glass baking dish and pour hot seasoned mixture over beef. Cover partially with plastic wrap and refrigerate for 3 days. Turn several times each day.

- Remove beef from baking dish and pat dry. Pour marinade into strainer over bowl and discard peppercorns and cloves. Add oil to large roasting pan, heat and brown beef on all sides. Transfer to plate.

- Add celery, carrots and onion to roasting pan and saute over medium heat until onion is translucent. Add flour and stir frequently over low heat until mixture thickens and becomes light brown.

- Pour strained marinade into roasting pan with ⅔ cup water; bring to a boil and reduce heat to low-medium. Add roast, cover and cook for about 1 hour 30 minutes or until meat is tender.

- Transfer roast to serving platter, cool slightly and cut thin slices. Pour remaining liquid in roasting pan into gravy boat and serve with roast. Serves 6 to 8.

Rosemary Roast Dinner

1 (4 - 5 pound) rump roast
Flour
¼ cup (½ stick) butter
1 tablespoon rosemary
1 tablespoon oregano
1 teaspoon seasoned salt
1 (10 ounce) can beef broth
1 cup brewed coffee
2 teaspoons minced garlic
6 potatoes, peeled, quartered
12 carrots, peeled
2 onions, quartered

- Preheat oven to 325°.

- Dredge roast in flour. Melt butter in large, heavy pan and brown roast on all sides.

- Add seasonings, broth, coffee and garlic and bake for 2 hours.

- Add vegetables and continue cooking for additional 1 hour. Serves 12.

German Pot Roast

1 (3 - 4 pound) rump roast
2 tablespoons canola oil
6 medium potatoes, peeled, quartered
6 medium carrots, quartered
3 medium onions, quartered

- Preheat oven to 350°.

- Brown roast in oil on all sides in large skillet over medium-high heat. Place in large roasting pan and season with a little salt and pepper. Add ¾ cup water to pan, cover and bake for 2 hours.

- Add vegetables, cover and bake for an additional 2 hours or until tender. Add water if needed. Serves 10.

Mom's Best Pot Roast

1 (4 - 5 pound) boneless rump roast
Seasoned salt
Seasoned pepper
Garlic powder
6 medium potatoes, peeled, quartered
8 carrots, peeled, quartered
3 onions, peeled, quartered

- Preheat oven to 375°.

- Set roast in roasting pan with lid and sprinkle liberally with seasoned salt, seasoned pepper and garlic powder.

- Add 2 cups water and bake for 30 minutes.

- Reduce heat to 325° and bake for 3 hours. Add potatoes, carrots and onions and bake for additional 40 to 45 minutes.

- Place roast on serving platter and place potatoes, carrots and onion around roast.

Gravy:

3 tablespoons cornstarch

- Combine cornstarch and ¾ cup water and add to juices remaining in roaster. Add ½ teaspoon each of salt and pepper.

- On stovetop, cook on high and stir constantly until gravy is thick.

- Serve in gravy boat with roast and vegetables. Serves 8.

Until the late 1600's, all pretzels were soft. The story goes that a baker's apprentice in Pennsylvania fell asleep and left the pretzels in the oven longer than usual. When the baker tried the crisp pretzel, he liked it and the new hard pretzel became widespread.

Slow Cooker Corned Beef Brisket

4 ribs celery, chopped
3 medium onions, quartered
1 (2 - 3 pound) corned beef brisket, trimmed
2 tablespoons whole black peppercorns
2 bay leaves
1 large head green cabbage, quartered
8 - 10 small red or new potatoes, quartered
10 - 12 small carrots
2 tablespoons butter, melted

- Place celery and onions in sprayed 5-quart slow cooker and place brisket on top. Sprinkle peppercorns and bay leaves on top of brisket and add 3 to 4 cups water.

- Cook on LOW for 8 to 9 hours or until brisket is fork-tender.

- Place brisket on platter and discard liquid. Let stand for 10 to 20 minutes before slicing.

- Place cabbage, potatoes, carrots and ¼ cup water in large microwave-safe bowl. Microwave on HIGH for about 7 minutes. Stir and rotate in microwave.

- Microwave again on HIGH for about 5 minutes or until vegetables are tender.

- Pour butter over vegetables, season with a little salt and pepper and arrange around corned beef on platter. Serve immediately. Serves 6 to 8.

The best farmland in Pennsylvania is located in Chester and Lancaster counties and in the Great Appalachian Valley. This land attracted settlement by Germans (Deutsch) who became known as the Pennsylvania Dutch.

Fat Albert's Corned Beef and Cabbage

1 (3 pound) trimmed, corned beef brisket, trimmed
1 small onion, quartered
2 tablespoons pickling spice
1 teaspoon minced garlic
2 cups baby carrots or 8 carrots, peeled
8 small new (red) potatoes
1 small head cabbage, cored

- Place brisket and 2 quarts water in 6-quart heavy pan.

- Add onion, pickling spice and garlic, cover and bring to a boil. Reduce heat to low, cover and simmer for 2 hours.

- Cut large carrots in 1½-inch pieces. Add carrots and potatoes to brisket and simmer for additional 30 minutes.

- Cut cabbage into 8 wedges and place on top of other ingredients; simmer for additional 15 minutes.

- Remove brisket and vegetables from pan and cool for several minutes before slicing brisket.

- Carve thin slices of brisket across the grain. Serve vegetables with brisket. Serves 8.

Bill Cosby was born in the Germantown neighborhood of Philadelphia in 1937.

Liver and Onions with Gravy

Bacon drippings or vegetable oil
1 pound calf liver, cut in serving size pieces
Flour
1 (10 ounce) can French onion soup
½ soup can water

- Heat bacon drippings or oil in large skillet over medium-high heat. Season liver with a little salt and pepper and dredge in flour. Brown both sides in skillet.

- Pour soup and water over liver and stir to loosen crumbs in skillet. Cover and reduce heat.

- Cook for about 15 to 20 minutes more or until gravy thickens. Serves 4.

Traditional Wiener Schnitzel

1½ pounds (½ inch) thick veal cutlets
½ cup flour
2 eggs, beaten
1 cup dry fine breadcrumbs
¾ cup (1½ sticks) butter
1 lemon, thinly sliced

- Pound cutlets to very thin. Add a little salt and pepper to flour in shallow bowl and stir. Dredge cutlets on both sides in flour.

- Dip in eggs and sprinkle breadcrumbs on both sides.

- Melt butter in large skillet and saute cutlets over low heat for about 5 to 7 minutes on each side.

- Remove from skillet and keep warm on oven-proof platter in oven at 250° until ready to serve.

- Serve with slices of lemon. Serves 4.

Bacon-Wrapped Chicken

6 boneless, skinless chicken breast halves
1 (8 ounce) carton whipped cream cheese with onion and chives
Butter
6 bacon strips

- Preheat oven to 375°.

- Flatten chicken to ½-inch thick. Spread 3 tablespoons cream cheese over each. Dot with butter and a little salt and roll. Wrap each with bacon strip.

- Place seam-side down in sprayed 9 x 13-inch baking dish. Bake uncovered for 40 to 45 minutes or until juices run clear. To brown, broil 6 inches from heat for about 3 minutes or until bacon is crisp. Serves 4 to 6.

Slow Cooker Broccoli Seasoned Chicken

1¼ cups rice
2 pounds boneless, skinless chicken breast halves
1 teaspoon dried parsley
1 (1.8 ounce) packet cream of broccoli soup mix
1 (14 ounce) can chicken broth

- Place rice in lightly sprayed slow cooker. Cut chicken into slices and place over rice.

- Sprinkle with parsley.

- Combine soup mix, chicken broth and 1 cup water in saucepan. Heat just enough to mix well. Pour over chicken and rice.

- Cover and cook on LOW for 6 to 8 hours. Serves 8.

Pennsylvania has 58,200 farms covering 7,700,000 acres. (2005)

It's Honey-Baked Chicken, Honey

2 whole chickens, quartered
½ cup (1 stick) butter, melted
⅔ cup honey
¼ cup dijon-style mustard
1 teaspoon curry powder

- Preheat oven to 350°.

- Place chicken pieces skin-side up in sprayed 10 x 15-inch baking dish and sprinkle with a little salt.

- Combine butter, honey, mustard and curry powder in bowl and pour over chicken.

- Bake for 1 hour 5 minutes and baste every 20 minutes. Serves 8.

Cranberry Chicken

6 boneless, skinless chicken breast halves
1 (16 ounce) can whole cranberry sauce
1 large tart apple, peeled, chopped
⅓ cup chopped walnuts
1 teaspoon curry powder

- Preheat oven to 350°.

- Place chicken in sprayed 9 x 13-inch baking pan and bake for 20 minutes.

- Combine cranberry sauce, apple, walnuts and curry powder in bowl and mix well; spoon over chicken.

- Bake for additional 25 minutes or until chicken juices run clear. Serves 6.

The first botanic garden in North America was established by John Bartram of Philadelphia in the 1720's. Bartram's Garden and the Bartram home are still maintained today.

Sweet-and-Sour Cranberry Chicken

1 (10 ounce) jar sweet-and-sour sauce
1 (1 ounce) packet onion soup mix
1 (16 ounce) can whole cranberry sauce
6 boneless, skinless chicken breast halves

- Preheat oven to 325°.

- Combine sweet-and-sour sauce, onion soup mix and cranberry sauce in bowl.

- Place chicken breasts in sprayed 9 x 13-inch shallow baking dish. Pour cranberry mixture over chicken breasts.

- Cover and bake for 30 minutes. Uncover and bake for additional 25 minutes or until juices run clear. Serves 6.

Oregano Chicken

¼ cup (½ stick) butter, melted
1 (.4 ounce) packet Italian salad dressing mix
2 tablespoons lemon juice
4 boneless, skinless chicken breast halves
2 tablespoons dried oregano

- Preheat oven to 350°.

- Combine butter, salad dressing mix and lemon juice in bowl.

- Place chicken in sprayed 9 x 13-inch baking pan. Spoon butter mixture over chicken.

- Cover and bake for 45 minutes. Uncover and baste with pan drippings and sprinkle with oregano.

- Bake for additional 15 minutes or until chicken juices run clear. Serves 4.

Old-Fashioned Chicken Pie

1 large chicken, cut up
2 cups flour
2 teaspoons baking powder
½ teaspoon baking soda
1 teaspoon sugar
6 tablespoons shortening
¾ cup buttermilk*
½ cup (1 stick) butter

- Preheat oven to 350°.

- Sprinkle salt and pepper over each piece of chicken. Place in sprayed 9 x 13-inch baking dish.

- Mix flour, baking powder, baking soda and sugar in bowl and cut in shortening a little at a time. Stir well. Pour buttermilk in gradually and mix well to form dough consistency.

- Roll dough on floured surface to make a very thin piecrust. Cut in strips of 1 inch wide. Lay strips over chicken and dot with butter.

- Add enough boiling water to barely cover chicken.

- Cover and bake for 1 hour 30 minutes. Add more boiling water if needed for the liquid in pie. Serves 6.

*TIP: To make buttermilk, mix 1 cup milk with 1 tablespoon lemon juice or vinegar and let milk stand for about 10 minutes.

The Jacktown Fair is the nation's oldest continuing fair, was established in 1865 and is held in Wind Ridge, Pennsylvania (Greene County) in mid-summer. Featuring crop and livestock competitions along with agricultural events such as horse pulls, this event lasts seven days. It's said, "You can't die happy till you've been to the Jacktown Fair!"

Easy Chicken Pot Pie

1 (15 ounce/2 piecrusts) package refrigerated piecrusts
1 (19 ounce) can cream of chicken soup
2 cups cooked, diced chicken breasts
1 (10 ounce) package frozen mixed vegetables, thawed

- Preheat oven to 325°.

- Place 1 piecrust in 9-inch deep-dish pie pan. Fill with chicken soup, chicken and mixed vegetables. Gently stir to mix.

- Cover with second piecrust, fold edges under and crimp. With knife, cut 4 slits in center of piecrust.

- Bake for 1 hour 15 minutes or until crust is golden brown. Serves 8.

TIP: *When you're too busy to cook a chicken, get rotisserie chicken from the grocery store. They are great.*

Maple-Plum Glazed Turkey Breast

2 cups red plum jam
1 cup maple syrup
1 teaspoon dry mustard
¼ cup lemon juice
1 (5 pound) bone-in turkey breast

- Combine all ingredients except turkey in saucepan. Bring to boiling point, turn heat down and simmer for about 20 minutes or until it thickens. Reserve 1 cup glaze.

- Place turkey breast in roasting pan and pour remaining glaze over turkey.

- Bake turkey according to package directions. Slice turkey and serve with reserved hot glaze. Serves 6 to 8.

Lamb Paprika

6 slices bacon
3 - 4 medium potatoes, chopped
2 medium onions, chopped
1 pound lamb, cubed
Flour
1 tablespoon paprika
½ teaspoon crushed fresh rosemary
½ teaspoon caraway seeds
3 medium tomatoes, chopped
½ cup red wine
½ cup beef broth

- Fry bacon in large skillet, drain on paper towel and crumble when cool. Saute potatoes and onions in bacon drippings until golden brown. Drain on paper towels.

- Coat lamb with flour and brown in remaining bacon drippings. Remove from heat and return potatoes and onions to skillet with lamb.

- Sprinkle paprika, rosemary, caraway seeds, and ½ teaspoon each of salt and pepper over mixture.

- Combine tomatoes, wine and broth and pour over lamb mixture, cover and cook over low heat for about 35 to 45 minutes. Serve hot. Serves 4.

The Clinton County Fair, located in Mackeyville, Pennsylvania has something for everyone. From all the interesting animal exhibits and competitions to baking and cooking contests including a chili cook-off, Hershey baked goods (a Pennsylvania tradition), apple pie and angel food cake. It's a nine-day event in midsummer.

Lamb Chops with Black Cherry Sauce

3 tablespoons flour
8 (1 inch) thick lamb rib chops
1 tablespoon butter
1 tablespoon olive oil
2 cups thinly sliced red onion
1 cup black cherry juice (unsweetened)
1 cup halved, pitted fresh black cherries or other dark cherries
⅓ cup sliced fresh basil, divided

- Preheat oven to 250°.

- Mix flour with ¾ teaspoon salt and ½ teaspoon pepper in shallow bowl. Dredge lamb chops in flour mixture and shake off excess.

- Melt butter with oil in large skillet over medium-high heat. Cook lamb chops for about 3 minutes per side for medium-rare, about 4 minutes per side for medium. Transfer chops to baking dish and place in oven to keep warm.

- In same skillet with drippings, add onion and sauté for about 2 minutes. Add cherry juice and bring to boil. Scrape browned bits off the bottom and sides of skillet. Continue boiling and until sauce is slightly reduced and onions are softened, about 4 minutes. Stir often.

- Add cherries and half basil and cook for 1 minute; add a little salt and pepper.

- Place lamb chops on 4 plates (2 per plate), pour sauce over chops and sprinkle with remaining basil. Serves 4.

Kane claims the title of Black Cherry Capital of the World. Its Black Cherry Festival is held for three days in July. Some 75% of the best quality cherries are grown within a 30-mile radius of Kane.

Macaroni-Ham Casserole

2 cups pasta shells
2 cups cooked, chopped ham
1 egg, beaten
½ cup milk

- Preheat oven to 325°.

- Cook pasta in salted water according to package directions. Drain well.

- Layer pasta and ham in sprayed 9 x 13-inch baking dish.

- Mix egg and milk in bowl and pour over casserole. Bake for 1 hour. Serve immediately. Serves 6.

Apricot-Baked Ham

1 (12 - 20 pound) whole ham, fully cooked, bone-in
Whole cloves
2 tablespoons dry mustard
1¼ cups apricot jam
1¼ cups packed light brown sugar

- Preheat oven to 450°.

- Trim skin and excess fat from ham. Place ham on rack in large roasting pan and insert cloves every inch or so. Be sure to push cloves into ham surface as far as they will go.

- Combine dry mustard and jam in bowl and spread over entire surface of ham. Pat brown sugar over jam mixture, reduce heat to 325° and bake uncovered for 15 minutes per pound. Sugary crust that forms on ham will seal the juices in the ham.

- When ham is done, remove from oven and set aside for 20 minutes before carving. Serves 10 to 12.

Schnitz un Knepp

(Ham, apples and dumplings) This hearty dish is a traditional favorite.

4 cups dried apples
1 (3 pound) smoked ham
2 tablespoons brown sugar

Dumplings:

2 cups flour
4 teaspoons baking powder
1 egg, well beaten
3 tablespoons butter, melted
½ cup milk

- Place apples in a pot and cover with water; soak at least 3 hours or overnight.

- In stock pot, cover ham with water and simmer for 2 hours. Add apples and the water in which they were soaked; bring to boil and simmer for 1 hour. Stir in brown sugar.

- Mix together flour, baking powder, 1 teaspoon salt and ¼ teaspoon pepper.

- In separate bowl, combine egg, butter and milk. Stir egg mixture into flour mixture all at once; mix just until it blends. Drop tablespoonfuls into simmering liquid with ham and apples. Cover pot tightly and simmer for 20 minutes until dumplings are done. Serves 8 to 10.

Pennsylvania is home to more than 2,300 food processing companies. It leads the country in the value of chocolate, canned fruit, vegetable specialty products, potato chips and pretzels.

Peach-Pineapple Baked Ham

1 (3 - 4) pound boneless, smoked ham
¼ cup dijon-style mustard, divided
1 cup peach preserves
1 cup pineapple preserves

- Preheat oven to 325°.

- Spread half mustard on ham. Place ham in sprayed shallow baking pan and bake for 20 minutes.

- Combine remaining mustard and preserves in microwave-safe bowl and heat in microwave for 20 seconds or in small saucepan on low heat for 2 to 3 minutes. Pour over ham and bake for about 15 minutes. Serves 8 to 10.

Stovetop Ham Supper

1 (12 ounce) package spiral pasta
3 tablespoons butter, sliced
2 - 3 cups cooked, cubed ham
1 teaspoon minced garlic
1 (16 ounce) package frozen broccoli, cauliflower and carrots
½ cup sour cream
1 (8 ounce) package shredded cheddar cheese, divided

- Preheat oven to 375°.

- Cook pasta in large saucepan, according to package directions, drain and stir in butter while still hot. Add ham, garlic and 1 teaspoon salt.

- Cook vegetables in microwave according to package directions and stir, with liquid, into pasta-ham mixture. Stir in sour cream and half cheese. Mix until they blend well.

- Spoon into sprayed 3-quart baking dish. Bake for 15 minutes or just until bubbly around edges. Sprinkle remaining cheese on top and let stand until cheese melts. Serves 6 to 8.

Saucy Ham Loaf

1 pound ham, ground
½ pound ground beef
½ pound ground pork
2 eggs
1 cup bread or cracker crumbs
2 teaspoons Worcestershire sauce
1 (5 ounce) can evaporated milk
3 tablespoons chili sauce
1 teaspoon seasoned salt
1 teaspoon seasoned pepper
Bacon strips for top of loaf, optional

- Preheat oven to 350°.

- Combine all ingredients except bacon. Form into loaf in sprayed 9 x 13-inch baking pan. Place bacon strips over top and bake for 1 hour. Serves 4 to 6.

TIP: *Have butcher grind all 3 meats together.*

Sweet-and-Hot Mustard:

4 ounces dry mustard
1 cup vinegar
3 eggs, beaten
1 cup sugar

- Combine mustard and vinegar in bowl until smooth and set aside overnight.

- Add eggs and sugar and cook in double boiler. Stir for 8 to 10 minutes or until mixture coats spoon.

- Cool and store in covered jars in refrigerator. Serve with ham loaf.

TIP: *The Sweet-and-Hot Mustard recipe also goes well on sandwiches.*

More than 6,000 Pennsylvanian farmers are women.

Grilled Ham and Apples

½ cup orange marmalade
1 tablespoon butter
¼ teaspoon ground ginger
1 (1 pound/½ inch) thick ham slice
2 apples, cut into ½-inch thick slices

- Combine marmalade, butter and ginger in 1-cup glass measuring cup. Microwave for 1 minute, stirring once.

- Place ham slices on grill and close grill lid.

- Grill for about 5 to 10 minutes, turn occasionally and baste with marmalade mixture.

- Place apple slices on ham and grill for additional 5 to 10 minutes. Serves 4 to 6.

Prize-Winning Pork Tenderloin

Marinade:

⅔ cup soy sauce
⅔ cup canola oil
2 tablespoons crystallized ginger, finely chopped
2 tablespoons fresh lime juice
1 teaspoon garlic powder
2 tablespoons minced onion

2 pork tenderloins

- Combine all marinade ingredients in bowl and pour over pork tenderloins. Marinate for about 36 hours.

- When ready to serve, cook over charcoal fire for about 45 minutes. Serves 8 to 10.

Sweet-and-Sour Pork Cutlets

¾ cup flour
4 (3 ounce) pork cutlets
2 tablespoons butter, divided
¾ cup orange juice
⅓ cup Craisins®
1 tablespoon dijon-style mustard
1 tablespoon brown sugar

* Place flour in shallow bowl and dredge cutlets in flour.

* Brown pork cutlets in heavy skillet with 1 tablespoon butter; turn once.

* Add orange juice, Craisins®, mustard, brown sugar and remaining butter.

* Cook on high until mixture bubbles. Reduce heat and simmer for about 5 minutes. Serves 4.

Pork Chops and Apples

6 thick-cut pork chops
Flour
Canola oil
3 baking apples

* Preheat oven to 325°.

* Dip pork chops in flour, coat well and brown in skillet with a little oil.

* Place in sprayed 9 x 13-inch baking dish. Add ⅓ cup water, cover and bake for 45 minutes.

* Peel, halve and seed apples. Place halves over each pork chop. Return to oven for 5 to 10 minutes. (Do NOT overcook apples.) Serves 6.

Old-Fashioned Scrapple

This is a famous traditional German recipe that was always made at hog slaughtering time with leftover bits of pork and broth. Nothing was wasted and every part of the hog was used. This is a modern version of Scrapple – but it's still old-fashioned.

1½ pounds pork bones
½ pound pork sausage
4 - 5 cloves garlic, minced
Cornmeal
Hot sauce
Canola oil

- Simmer bones, sausage and garlic in 1 gallon water in large stock pot for about 2 hours. Discard bones and pour liquid through strainer into large bowl. Allow liquid to cool and skim fat from top.

- Measure liquid and return to pot with sausage and any strained slivers of meat. Over low heat slowly add 1¼ cups cornmeal to pot for each quart liquid and stir well. Stir out any lumps.

- Add a little salt, pepper and hot sauce. Bring to a boil gradually and stir constantly. Pour mixture into sprayed 9 x 13-inch baking dish and refrigerate uncovered overnight.

- Cut into ½-inch slices and fry in a little oil until brown on both sides. Serves 10 to 12.

TIP: If you don't have time to refrigerate overnight, form into patties before frying.

Pittsburgh was originally named Pittsbourg in honor of a British prime minister, William Pitt. The current spelling was adopted in 1794. The Post Office advocated the use of "burg" to simplify the spelling of place names. Pittsburgh, however, fought to keep the "h" at the end of its name and so today it is the most often misspelled city name in the nation.

Sauerkraut and Kielbasa

2 (16 ounce) cans sauerkraut
2 (12 ounce) cans beer
1 tablespoon light brown sugar
1 (1 pound) package kielbasa sausage, sliced

- Wash sauerkraut thoroughly and drain in colander. Place in large saucepan and pour beer over top. (Make sure beer more than covers sauerkraut.) Add brown sugar and stir.

- Cook over high heat until it boils. Reduce heat and simmer on low for 1 hour 15 minutes.

- Place sausage in sauerkraut and cook for an additional 15 to 20 minutes. Drain sauerkraut and serve hot. Serves 4.

Baked River Fish

1 pound fish fillets
3 tablespoons plus ¼ cup butter, divided
1 teaspoon tarragon
2 teaspoons capers
2 tablespoons lemon juice

- Preheat oven to 375°.

- Place fish fillets with 3 tablespoons butter in sprayed shallow pan and sprinkle with salt and pepper.

- Bake for about 6 to 8 minutes, turn and bake until fish flakes. (Do not overcook.)

- For sauce, melt ¼ cup butter with tarragon, capers and lemon juice in saucepan and serve over warm fish. Serves 4 to 6.

Held in Dunbar, Pennsylvania every summer, the Fayette County Fair is one of the largest in Pennsylvania with attendance of nearly 100,000. There's fun for the family with kids' activities as well as livestock and agricultural contests and exhibits.

Rainbow Trout Skillet

2 (1 pound) rainbow trout fillets
½ cup (1 stick) plus 3 tablespoons butter, divided
10 - 12 large cloves garlic, minced
3 small green onions with tops, minced
3 tablespoons white wine
1 egg, lightly beaten
1 - 3 tablespoons canola oil
1 lemon, sliced

- Wash and pat dry trout fillets and set aside.

- Melt ½ cup butter in skillet and saute garlic and green onions over medium heat until they are translucent. Add white wine and simmer while fish cooks.

- Beat egg slightly with 1 tablespoon water in bowl and dip each fillet into egg mixture.

- In separate skillet, heat a little oil and 1 tablespoon butter and place fillets to cook over medium heat.

- Turn once, add 1 to 2 tablespoons butter, if needed, and remove when fish flakes in thickest part.

- Arrange on platter, keep fish warm and pour warm garlic sauce over fish just before serving. Garnish with lemon slices. Serves 2.

In 1751, the Speaker of the Pennsylvania Assembly ordered a new bell from England for the statehouse. He asked that a Bible verse to be placed on the bell: "Proclaim LIBERTY throughout all the Land unto all the inhabitants thereof" (Leviticus 25:10). It cracked soon after it arrived in Philadelphia and it was recast by local craftsmen, using the metal from the original bell. It was rung on July 8, 1776, to summon the citizens of Philadelpha to hear the first public reading of the Declaration of Independence. The bell cracked again in the 19th century and is on display in Philadelphia today.

Brook Trout Wrapped in Foil

1 onion, sliced
1 rib celery, chopped
1 carrot, chopped
¼ teaspoon thyme
1 bay leaf
3 sprigs parsley, snipped
2 (12 ounce) brook trout, dressed
½ cup white wine
2 teaspoons butter
⅓ cup half-and-half cream
2 teaspoons flour

- Preheat oven to 400°.

- Make pouch out of heavy-duty foil large enough for vegetables and fish.

- Place onion, celery, carrot, thyme, bay leaf and parsley on first. Place trout on top and pour wine over fish.

- Seal foil pouch so no liquids escape. Place in sprayed baking dish and cook for about 20 to 30 minutes until fish flakes, but is not dry.

- A few minutes before fish is ready, melt butter in saucepan over low heat. Add half-and-half cream and flour slowly and whisk to dissolve lumps. Remove from heat and pour liquid from pouch into saucepan.

- Whisk into sauce, add vegetables and pour over fish. Serve immediately. Serves 3 to 4.

The official state fish of Pennsylvania is the Brook Trout. Pennsylvania's many streams and rivers attract sport fishermen with a number of species of fish.

Homemade Salmon Patties

1 (7 ounce) can pink salmon
½ cup fine breadcrumbs
2 egg whites
2 tablespoons diced onion
2 tablespoons chopped fresh parsley
1 tablespoon lemon juice
1 tablespoon canola oil
Lemon wedges

- Drain salmon and set aside liquid. Place salmon in bowl and mash with fork. Combine with breadcrumbs, egg whites, onion, parsley and lemon juice. Add ¼ teaspoon pepper. Add 2 or 3 tablespoons salmon liquid.

- Mix well and shape into patties. Fry patties in oil over medium heat until light brown on both sides. Serve with lemon wedges. Serves 4.

Deep-Fried Shrimp

1 cup milk
2 eggs, beaten
1½ cups flour
2 teaspoons seasoned salt
About 40 saltine crackers, finely crushed
1 - 1½ pounds medium shrimp, peeled, veined
Canola oil
Cocktail sauce

- Combine milk and eggs in shallow bowl.

- In separate shallow bowl, combine flour and seasoned salt. Place cracker crumbs in third shallow bowl.

- Dip shrimp in flour mixture, then in milk-egg mixture and finally in cracker crumbs and cover well.

- Deep-fry shrimp in oil until golden brown and serve with cocktail sauce. Serves 4.

Seaside Oyster Loaf

2 (8 ounce) packages cream cheese, softened
⅔ cup mayonnaise
1 teaspoon hot pepper sauce
2 tablespoons Worcestershire sauce
1 tablespoon milk
2 tablespoons seasoned breadcrumbs
2 (4 ounce) cans smoked oysters, drained, chopped
Parsley

- Beat cream cheese, mayonnaise, hot pepper sauce, Worcestershire sauce, milk and breadcrumbs in bowl. (If mixture is not pliable, add a little more milk.)

- Stir in oysters and place in sprayed 9 x 5-inch loaf pan. Refrigerate for several hours before serving. Garnish with parsley. Serves 4.

Scalloped Oysters

1 cup dry breadcrumbs
2 cups cracker crumbs
1 cup (2 sticks) butter, melted
1 (1 quart) carton oysters with liquor
¼ cup cream

- Preheat oven to 400°.

- Mix bread and cracker crumbs in bowl. Stir butter into crumbs. Place one-third crumb mixture in sprayed 7 x 11-inch baking dish.

- Drain liquor from oysters and set aside. Cover crumb mixture with half oysters. Sprinkle with a little salt and pepper. Add half oyster liquor and cream. Cover with half remaining crumbs. Repeat.

- Bake for 30 minutes. Serves 4 to 6.

Allegheny Backstrap

Backstrap is the tenderloin of venison and the very best part.

3 - 4 pound venison backstrap, sliced
Milk
1½ cups flour
Canola oil
2 cups milk or half-and-half cream

- Place backstrap in bowl and cover with milk. Soak in refrigerator for several hours or overnight.

- Remove from milk and cut into ¼-inch slices.

- Combine flour, 1 teaspoon salt and ½ teaspoon pepper in shallow bowl and dredge each backstrap slice in flour mixture.

- Cook in oil in skillet on medium heat until slices are light brown.

- For gravy, use 2 tablespoons of the remaining seasoned flour and brown in skillet with pan drippings.

- Pour in milk or half-and-half cream; stir constantly and cook until gravy thickens.

- If gravy is too thick, add a little more milk. Serves 6 to 8.

Whitetail deer (the state mammal), black bear, turkey, ruffed grouse (the state bird), pheasant, wild boar and other wildlife are hunted in Pennsylvania. There are also a limited number of elk hunts.

Chicken-Fried Venison Steak and Pan Gravy

2 pounds venison steak, tenderized, thinly sliced
1 cup flour
Canola oil

- Season venison with a little salt and pepper. Dredge all steak pieces in flour until well coated.

- Heat about ½ inch oil in heavy skillet and fry steak pieces until golden brown.

- Remove from skillet and drain on paper towels.

Pan gravy:

6 tablespoons flour
6 - 8 tablespoons pan drippings
3 cups milk

- Move steaks to warm oven. Add flour to drippings in skillet, stir constantly and cook until flour begins to brown.

- Add ½ teaspoon salt and ¼ teaspoon pepper; add milk slowly and stir until gravy thickens.

- Serve in bowl or over steaks. Serves 6 to 8.

TIP: Bacon drippings make better cream gravy, but it is good just about any way you fix it.

Representative of Pennsylvania's dairy industry, milk is the official state beverage.

Marinated Venison Roast

This is great for appetizers or snacks anytime. It's a terrific recipe for venison.

2 - 3 pounds venison roast, cooked
3 onions, sliced in rings
8 - 10 fresh mushrooms, halved
2 (3 ounce) jars capers, drained
¼ cup red wine vinegar
¾ cup canola oil
1 teaspoon sugar

- Cut venison into bite-size pieces.

- Layer venison, onions, mushrooms and capers in large bowl.

- In separate bowl, mix vinegar, oil, sugar, and ½ teaspoon each of salt and pepper and mix well.

- Pour over venison and mix additional amounts of red wine vinegar, oil, sugar, salt and pepper as needed to cover venison.

- Cover and marinate for at least 1 to 2 days before serving. Stir occasionally. Serves 6 to 8.

TIP: Cooking Venison Roast: The best way to cook a roast or ham for this recipe is to season it liberally with salt and pepper. Place in roasting pan and add 1 to 2 cups water. Bake at 300° for about 3 to 4 hours or until fork-tender. Check to make sure there is enough water and venison does not dry out.

Held annually in Kennett Square, Pennsylvania in the early fall, the two-day Mushroom Festival celebrates Kennett Square's prominence as the "Mushroom Capital of the World". Replete with cooking demonstrations, food, children's activities, farm tours and entertainment, the event attracts over 100,000 visitors each year.

Deer Camp Stew

1 (28 ounce) can Mexican stewed tomatoes
2 (15 ounce) cans beef broth
2 - 3 pounds venison, cubed
Bacon drippings or canola oil
1 (6 ounce) bottle Worcestershire sauce
2 - 3 teaspoons paprika
5 - 6 potatoes, chopped
3 - 4 large onions, chopped
1 (16 ounce) bag baby carrots, sliced
3 - 4 ribs celery, chopped

- Pour tomatoes and beef broth into large stew pot and turn heat to warm.

- Brown venison in bacon drippings in large skillet. Pour venison and pan drippings into stew pot.

- Add Worcestershire sauce, paprika, and 2 teaspoons each of salt and pepper.

- Bring stew to a boil, reduce heat to low and cook for 2 to 3 hours or until venison is fairly tender.

- Add potatoes, onions and carrots and cook on low heat for additional 1 to 2 hours. Adjust seasonings to taste as stew cooks.

- Add celery about 15 to 20 minutes before serving to give stew a little crunch. Serves 8 to 10.

Born in Texas and raised in Missouri, the 34th President of the United States (1953-1961), Dwight D. Eisenhower (1890-1969), chose Gettysburg, Pennsylvania as both a getaway retreat and his retirement home. The farm is now known as the Eisenhower National Historic Site.

Venison Jerky

2 tablespoons vinegar
2 tablespoons steak sauce
1 teaspoon liquid smoke
1 teaspoon garlic salt
1 onion, minced
2 - 3 pounds venison

- Mix vinegar, steak sauce, liquid smoke, garlic salt and ½ teaspoon pepper in large bowl and whisk thoroughly. Add onion to marinade and set aside.

- Cut venison into strips about ¼-inch thick and about 1 inch wide.

- Add venison to marinade and mix well. Make sure all venison is covered with marinade. Seal and store in refrigerator for 24 hours.

- When ready to bake, preheat oven to 200°.

- Remove from refrigerator; drain venison strips and place on baking sheet with space in between all pieces.

- Bake for about 5 hours. Turn once or twice while cooking. Serves 8 to 12.

America's 15th President (1857-1861), James Buchanan, was born April 13, 1791, in Cove Gap, Pennsylvania, and died June 1, 1868, at his Wheatland estate located near Lancaster. Wheatland is now a museum.

Hasenpfeffer

(Stewed Rabbit)

Flour
8 - 10 slices of dressed rabbit
¼ cup bacon drippings
2 medium onions, sliced
2 cloves garlic, minced
½ teaspoon ground cloves
2 bay leaves
½ cup vinegar
1 (15 ounce) can stewed tomatoes
1 (10 ounce) can tomato puree
Fresh mushrooms, sliced, optional

- Preheat oven to 350°.

- Mix flour with 1 teaspoon salt and ¼ teaspoon pepper in shallow bowl. Dredge rabbit slices in flour mixture and fry in hot bacon drippings until golden brown.

- Place rabbit slices in 2½-quart baking dish and add onions, garlic, cloves, bay leaves, vinegar, stewed tomatoes, tomato puree and mushrooms (if desired).

- Bake for 1 to 1½ hours. Remove bay leaves before serving. Serves 8 to 10.

Agaricus (button) mushrooms are grown mainly in Chester County as are specialty mushrooms like shiitake and oyster mushrooms.

Fancy Fried Game Birds

1 (6 ounce) can frozen orange juice concentrate, thawed
1 teaspoon lemon juice
10 - 12 quail or doves
1 - 2 cups biscuit mix
Canola oil

- Combine orange juice concentrate, lemon juice and ½ teaspoon salt in large shallow bowl.

- Place birds in bowl with marinade, add enough water to cover birds and marinate for 2 to 3 hours. Discard marinade.

- Pour biscuit mix in shallow bowl and dredge birds in biscuit mix to cover well.

- Fry birds in heated, deep-fat fryer until light brown. Drain on paper towels and serve hot. Serves 5 to 6.

Fried Dove and Gravy

2 eggs, beaten
⅓ cup plus 1 - 2 cups milk, divided
1 - 1½ cups flour
½ teaspoon seasoned salt
10 - 12 doves
Canola oil

- Combine eggs and ⅓ cup milk in shallow bowl.

- In separate shallow bowl, combine flour, seasoned salt and ½ teaspoon pepper. Dredge each dove in seasoned flour, dip in egg-milk mixture and again in flour mixture.

- Brown doves slowly in skillet with a little oil. Drain doves on paper towels.

- To make gravy, do not wash skillet and add 2 tablespoons remaining flour. Brown flour on medium heat until golden brown and add milk, stirring constantly until gravy thickens. Serve over mashed potatoes or biscuits or both. Serves 4 to 5.

Baked Quail

Some cooks think that if it has wings, you should fry it. Here's a good recipe to try when you don't want to fry the hunter's prize.

2 bunches green onions with tops, chopped
2 tablespoons butter, divided
⅔ cup flour
8 quail
1 (10 ounce) can cream of chicken soup
½ cup cream sherry

- Preheat oven to 225°.

- Saute green onions in 1 tablespoon butter in skillet and remove to plate.

- Combine a little salt and pepper and flour and dip quail in flour mixture, coating well.

- Brown quail in skillet with remaining butter. Transfer quail to sprayed shallow baking dish.

- Return onions to skillet, add soup and sherry and mix while cooking on medium heat.

- Pour mixture over quail, cover tightly and bake for 2 hours. Serves 4 to 5.

The Lawrence County Fair is a six-day fair in New Castle, Pennsylvania and has been held for more than 50 years. It is known for presenting one of the finest livestock shows in the Midwest. It includes crops, fruits and vegetables contests, crafts, entertainment and events for the whole family.

Baked Quail in Cream Sauce

6 - 8 quail
Flour
3 tablespoons butter
½ cup finely chopped fresh mushrooms
½ cup chopped fresh green onions
1 tablespoon chopped fresh parsley
⅔ cup white wine
⅔ cup whipping cream
Rice, cooked

- Preheat oven to 325°.

- Sprinkle quail with a little salt and pepper, roll in flour and coat well.

- Melt butter in skillet and lightly brown quail. Transfer to sprayed baking dish.

- Saute mushrooms and green onions in same skillet and add a little more butter, if necessary. Add parsley and white wine and pour over quail.

- Cover and bake for 45 to 50 minutes, basting twice.

- Add whipping cream and cook for additional 10 minutes. Serve over rice. Serves 4.

TIP: Use this recipe for cooking doves as well.

The Phillips Mushroom Museum is located in Kennett Square. Its displays illustrate three generations of mushroom farming by the Phillips family.

Honey Duck or Duck, Honey

½ teaspoon dried rosemary
½ teaspoon thyme
½ teaspoon marjoram
½ teaspoon ground dill
½ teaspoon chervil
¼ cup orange juice
2 (2 - 3 pound) ducks, dressed
½ cup honey, heated
Coarsely ground black pepper

- Mix rosemary, thyme, marjoram, dill and chervil in small bowl with orange juice.

- Cut ducks in half and cut several small slits on all sides.

- Cover ducks with honey and rosemary seasoning mix. Sprinkle with ½ teaspoon salt and liberally with black pepper. Set aside for about 1 hour for seasonings to flavor duck.

- When ready to bake, preheat oven to 400°.

- Place duck in roasting pan and roast for about 45 minutes to 1 hour. Outside of duck should be crispy and inside tender. Serves 6.

With a history of fairs going back to 1798, Washington County has a deep agricultural heritage expressed in friendly competition in events from cooking to horse racing with many livestock and agricultural exhibits and contests. It's great family fun with plenty of live entertainment, too, in this eight-day event usually held in August in Washington, Pennsylvania.

Baked Pheasant with Sweet-and-Sour Sauce

2 pheasants or ducks, cut up
¼ cup (½ stick) butter, melted
1 (15 ounce) can dark sweet cherries, drained
1 (15 ounce) can peach slices, drained
1 (8 ounce) bottle sweet-and-sour sauce
½ cup chili sauce
½ cup chopped onion
Rice, cooked

- Preheat oven to 325°. Place pheasants or ducks in sprayed 7 x 11-inch or 9 x 13-inch baking dish and drizzle butter over birds.

- Mix cherries, peach slices, sweet-and-sour sauce, chili sauce and onion in bowl and pour over birds. Bake for about 50 minutes or until birds are tender. Serve over rice. Serves 4 to 5.

TIP: This also works very well with dove and quail. Halve about 12 birds and follow the same procedure.

The ruffed grouse became the official state bird of Pennsylvania in 1931. Grouse live throughout Pennsylvania where the habitat is suitable.

Charcoal-Grilled Pheasant

Marinade:

½ cup canola oil
¼ cup white wine
3 tablespoons Worcestershire sauce
1 tablespoon vinegar
1 teaspoon sugar
½ - 1 teaspoon cracked black pepper
2 cloves garlic, minced
¼ cup minced onion

2 (2 pound) dressed pheasants, halved

- Combine all ingredients for marinade in flat glass dish and mix well.

- Place pheasant halves in dish and marinate for 3 hours. Drain and discard marinade.

- Sear outside of birds over medium high heat on charcoal or gas grill for several minutes. Move to low heat and grill birds for about 5 to 8 minutes or until juices run clear. Serves 3 to 4.

The Kaystone State is Pennsylvania's best known nickname. Its origin is cloudy, but many believe that because Pennsylvania's vote for independence was key to the new nation's formation, it became known as the Keystone State. Other nicknames include: the Quaker State, the Oil State, the Coal State and the Steel State.

Wild Turkey Breasts

This is a real delicacy and hunters really look forward to this meal.

Dressed wild turkey breasts
Freshly ground black pepper
Flour
Milk
Canola oil

- Slice turkey breasts in thin strips across the grain.

- Season with a little salt and generously with black pepper. Dip both sides in flour, dip in milk and again in flour.

- Place in large, heavy skillet with hot oil and cook on both sides until golden brown. Do not overcook. Drain on paper towels and serve immediately.

Titusville, Pennsylvania was the location of the world's first oil well. Prior to this well, oil had been collected where it seeped naturally from the earth. While oil was recognized as valuable, the supply was limited. The modern petroleum industry was launched when Edwin L. Drake drilled the first commercially successful oil well in 1859. Today the Drake Well Museum in Titusville commemorates this event and the history of petroleum production.

Sweets

Cakes
Pies & Cobblers
Cookies & Bars
Candy
Desserts

State Flower: *Mountain Laurel*

State Tree: *Eastern Hemlock*

State Beautification and Conservation Plant: *Penngift Crownvetch*

Yummy Dutch Apple Cake

4 apples, peeled, chopped
2¾ cups sugar, divided
1½ teaspoons ground cinnamon, divided
1½ teaspoons baking powder
1 cup shortening
3 eggs
½ teaspoon vanilla
1 yeast cake
1 cup milk
4 cups flour

- Preheat oven to 350°.

- Place apples, ½ cup sugar and ½ teaspoon cinnamon to large saucepan with enough water to cover apples and cook until apples are tender. Drain and set aside.

- Cream 2¼ cups sugar, baking powder and shortening in large bowl; add eggs, one at a time, and vanilla and stir well. Dissolve yeast cake in milk and add to sugar mixture.

- Add flour and remaining cinnamon a little at a time and mix well.

- Pour mixture into sprayed, floured 9 x 13-inch baking pan. Spread apples over top of cake.

- Bake for about 30 minutes or until toothpick inserted in center comes out clean. Let stand for 15 minutes before serving. Serves 8 to 10.

Held in the fall in Lahaska, Pennsylvania the Apple Festival features a medley of apple butter, apple cider, apple fritters, apples dipped in caramel, apple dumplings and fresh apples along with crafts, entertainment, pie-eating contests and bushels of fun!

The Best Fresh Apple Cake

1½ cups canola oil
2 cups sugar
3 eggs
2½ cups flour
½ teaspoon baking soda
2 teaspoons baking powder
½ teaspoon ground cinnamon
1 teaspoon vanilla
3 cups peeled, grated apples
1 cup chopped pecans

- Preheat oven to 350°.

- Mix oil, sugar and eggs in bowl and beat well.

- In separate bowl, combine flour, ½ teaspoon salt, baking soda, baking powder and cinnamon. Gradually add flour mixture to sugar-egg mixture.

- Add vanilla and fold in apples and pecans. Pour into sprayed, floured tube pan.

- Bake for 1 hour. While cake is still warm, invert onto serving plate.

Glaze:

2 tablespoons butter, melted
2 tablespoons milk
1 cup powdered sugar
1 teaspoon vanilla
¼ teaspoon lemon extract

- Combine butter, milk, powdered sugar, vanilla and lemon extract in bowl; mix well.

- Drizzle over cake while cake is still warm. Serves 18 to 20.

Pennsylvania is the only one of the 13 original colonies that does not have a coastline on the Atlantic Ocean.

Apple-Date-Walnut Cake

2 cups sugar
1½ cups canola oil
3 eggs
2 teaspoons vanilla
2½ cups flour
1 teaspoon baking soda
1½ teaspoons ground cinnamon
¼ teaspoon ground ginger
3 cups chopped apples
1 (8 ounce) package chopped dates
1 cup chopped walnuts

- Preheat oven to 325°.

- Blend sugar, oil, eggs and vanilla in bowl and beat well. Add flour, baking soda, ½ teaspoon salt, cinnamon and ginger and beat well. Fold in apples, dates and walnuts.

- Pour into sprayed, floured 10-inch tube pan and bake for 1 hour 30 minutes or until toothpick inserted in center comes out clean.

Glaze:

1 cup sugar
1 teaspoon almond extract

- Right before cake is done, bring sugar and 1⅓ cups water in saucepan to a rolling boil and stir constantly. Remove from heat and add almond extract.

- Pour glaze over hot cake. Set aside for 20 minutes before removing from pan. Serves 18 to 20.

Pennsylvania is one of the leading producers of eggs in the United States.

Applesauce Cake

½ cup shortening
1½ cups packed brown sugar
1 egg
1 teaspoon baking soda
1 cup thick applesauce
1 teaspoon ground cinnamon
½ teaspoon ground cloves
1½ - 2 cups flour

- Preheat oven to 350°.

- Cream shortening, brown sugar and egg in bowl.

- In separate bowl, dissolve baking soda in applesauce and add to shortening mixture.

- Sift 1 teaspoon salt, cinnamon and cloves with part of flour and add to shortening mixture.

- Add enough additional flour to make a fairly stiff batter.

- Pour batter into sprayed, floured loaf pan and bake for 50 to 60 minutes. Serves 6 to 8.

TIP: For additional flavor, add 1 cup raisins to batter.

Betsy Ross made the first American flag in Philadelphia. The family tradition recounts a visit from George Washington, George Ross and Robert Morris of the Continental Congress in June 1777 to request a flag with 13 stripes and 13 stars arranged in a circle in a field of blue. It is said that George Washington stated the circle of stars was created so that no colony could believe it was placed above another.

Old-Fashioned Buttermilk Cake

Don't worry about buying buttermilk. Check out the TIP below and you won't have to make a special trip to the grocery store.

1 cup buttermilk*
3 tablespoons vanilla
½ teaspoon baking soda
1 cup shortening
2 cups sugar
4 eggs
3 cups flour
¾ cup chopped walnuts

- Preheat oven to 325°.

- Pour buttermilk, vanilla and baking soda in glass and set aside.

- Place shortening in large bowl and cream until smooth. Add sugar slowly and continue to cream until mixture is fluffy.

- Add eggs one at a time and beat after each addition. Add buttermilk mixture and beat. When mixture is fluffy, gradually add flour and 1 teaspoon salt a little at a time and stir well after each addition. Fold in nuts.

- Pour into sprayed, floured 10-inch tube pan.

- Bake for about 1 hour or until toothpick inserted in center comes out clean. Serves 18 to 20.

*TIP: To make buttermilk, mix 1 cup milk with 1 tablespoon lemon juice or vinegar and let milk stand for about 10 minutes.

One in seven jobs in Pennsylvania is related to agriculture or food processing.

Pumpkin-Chess Cake

1 (18 ounce) box yellow cake mix
¾ cup (1½ sticks) butter, softened, divided
4 eggs, divided
1 (15 ounce) can pumpkin
2 teaspoons ground cinnamon
½ cup packed brown sugar
⅔ cup milk
½ cup sugar
⅔ cup chopped pecans

- Preheat oven to 350°.

- Set aside 1 cup cake mix. Mix rest of cake mix, ½ cup (1 stick) butter and 1 egg and press into sprayed, floured 9 x 13-inch baking pan.

- Mix pumpkin, 3 eggs, cinnamon, brown sugar and milk in bowl and pour over batter in pan.

- Use remaining cake mix, sugar, remaining butter and pecans to make topping and crumble over cake.

- Bake for 1 hour. Serves 10 to 12.

The Great Dane is the official state dog of Pennsylvania. On August 15, 1965, the Speaker of the Assembly called for a voice vote for designating the Great Dane as state dog. He was answered by barks, growls and yips, so he declared that the "arfs have it". This is now known as the "Barking Dog Vote". The Great Dane's history as a hunting and working dog in frontier Pennsylvania is illustrated by a portrait of William Penn with his Great Dane which hangs in the Governor's Reception Room in the Capitol in Harrisburg.

Old-Fashioned Pumpkin Pie Pound Cake

1 cup shortening
1¼ cups sugar
¾ cup packed brown sugar
5 eggs, room temperature
1 cup canned pumpkin
2½ cups flour
2 teaspoons ground cinnamon
1 teaspoon ground nutmeg
1 teaspoon baking soda
½ cup orange juice, room temperature
2 teaspoons vanilla
1½ cups chopped pecans

- Preheat oven to 325°.

- Cream shortening, sugar and brown sugar in bowl for about 4 minutes. Add eggs, one at a time and mix well after each addition. Blend in pumpkin.

- In separate bowl, mix flour, cinnamon, nutmeg, ¼ teaspoon salt and baking soda and mix well. Gradually beat dry ingredients into batter until ingredients mix well.

- Fold in orange juice, vanilla and pecans. Pour into sprayed, floured bundt pan.

- Bake for 1 hour 10 minutes to 1 hour 15 minutes or until toothpick inserted in center comes out clean. Allow cake to stand in pan for about 15 minutes. Turn cake out onto rack to cool completely before frosting.

Frosting:

1 (1 pound) box powdered sugar
6 tablespoons (¾ stick) butter, melted
¼ teaspoon orange extract
2 tablespoons orange juice

- Thoroughly mix powdered sugar, butter, orange extract and orange juice in bowl. Add more orange juice if frosting seems too stiff. Serves 18 to 20.

Strawberry Angel Delight Cake

1 cup sweetened condensed milk
¼ cup lemon juice
1 pint fresh strawberries, halved
1 prepared angel food cake
1 (1 pint) carton whipping cream, whipped
Strawberries for garnish

- Combine sweetened condensed milk and lemon juice in bowl. Fold in strawberries.

- Slice cake in half horizontally. Spread strawberry filling on bottom layer and place top layer over filling.

- Cover with whipped cream and top with extra strawberries. Serves 16.

Great Coconut Cake Deluxe

This cake is really moist and delicious and can be frozen if you need to make it in advance.

1 (18 ounce) box yellow cake mix
1 (14 ounce) can sweetened condensed milk
1 (15 ounce) can cream of coconut (not coconut milk)
1 (3 ounce) can flaked coconut
1 (8 ounce) carton whipped topping, thawed

- Preheat oven to 350°.

- Prepare cake mix according to package directions and pour into sprayed, floured 9 x 13-inch baking pan. Bake for 30 to 35 minutes or until toothpick inserted in center comes out clean.

- While cake is warm, punch holes in cake about 2 inches apart. Pour sweetened condensed milk over cake and spread around until all milk soaks into cake.

- Pour cream of coconut over cake and sprinkle coconut over top. Cool and frost with whipped topping. Serves 12 to 15.

Down Home Molasses Cake

½ cup shortening
½ cup sugar
3 eggs, separated
¾ teaspoon baking soda
⅔ cup molasses
2¼ cups flour, plus additional flour for dredging raisins
1 teaspoon ground cinnamon
¼ teaspoon ground cloves
¼ teaspoon ground mace
½ cup milk
½ cup raisins

- Preheat oven to 350°.

- Cream shortening, sugar and egg yolks in bowl.

- In separate bowl, combine baking soda with molasses and add to shortening mixture.

- Sift flour with cinnamon, cloves, mace and 1 teaspoon salt. Add alternately with milk to shortening mixture.

- Beat egg whites and fold into batter.

- Dredge raisins lightly with flour and stir lightly into batter.

- Pour batter into sprayed, floured loaf pan and bake for 50 to 60 minutes. Serves 6 to 8.

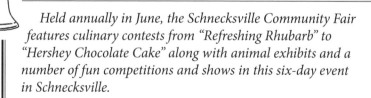

Held annually in June, the Schnecksville Community Fair features culinary contests from "Refreshing Rhubarb" to "Hershey Chocolate Cake" along with animal exhibits and a number of fun competitions and shows in this six-day event in Schnecksville.

Philly's Angel Food Cake

1 cup sifted flour
1¼ cups sugar, divided
8 egg whites
¾ teaspoon cream of tartar
1 teaspoon vanilla

- Preheat oven to 325°.

- Sift flour and ¾ cup sugar several times.

- Beat egg whites with ½ teaspoon salt in bowl until frothy. Add cream of tartar and beat until peaks form.

- Fold remaining sugar iinto meringue. Then gently and gradually fold in flour mixture.

- When it is partly blended, add vanilla. Use gentle folding motion to mix. (Stirring tends to release air that is needed for leavening.)

- Bake in sprayed, floured tube pan for 1 hour.

- After baking, invert cake, but do not remove from pan until almost cold. Serves 18 to 20.

One of the most remarkable of our Founding Fathers, Benjamin Franklin (1706-1790) was born in Boston, Massachusetts. He first came to Philadelphia, Pennsylvania at the age of 16 and set up shop there as a printer. He was elected to the Continental Congress in 1776. He was a signer of the Declaration of Independence, served as Commissioner to France and was a negotiator for the treaties with Great Britain, ending the Revolutionary War. He was president of the Pennsylvania Society for the Abolition of Slavery and was a senior member of the U.S. Constitutional Convention in 1785. He is buried in Christ Church Burial Ground in Philadelphia.

Fun Funnel Cakes

Vendors at fairs and festivals make lots of funnel cakes and everyone has one before they leave. You can tell who just ate one by the powdered sugar around their mouths.

1⅔ cups flour
¾ teaspoon baking soda
½ teaspoon cream of tartar
2 tablespoons sugar
1 cup milk
1 egg
Canola oil
¼ cup powdered sugar

- Mix flour, baking soda, cream of tartar, sugar and ¼ teaspoon salt in large bowl.

- In separate bowl, beat milk and egg. Pour into dry mixture and beat until smooth and creamy.

- Heat several inches of oil in large skillet. Pour ¾ cup batter into funnel while holding funnel closed with a fingertip. When oil is hot enough, remove finger from hole and let batter stream through funnel. Make circular motions with funnel so batter crosses and overlaps itself forming a lattice pattern.

- Fry until golden brown, flip and brown other side. Drain on paper towels and sprinkle with powdered sugar. Eat immediately. Serves about 8.

Held in Hughesville, Pennsylvania the Lycoming County Fair is a six-day fair in mid-summer and is filled with every kind of livestock and food exhibitions and competitions along with arts and crafts. People have gathered for this event every year for more than 130 years.

Spiced Cupcakes

½ cup shortening
1 cup sugar
2 eggs, separated
⅓ cup chopped, seeded raisins
⅓ cup chopped currants
⅓ cup chopped nuts
1 teaspoon baking soda
2½ cups flour
½ teaspoon ground cloves
½ teaspoon ground mace
1½ teaspoons ground cinnamon
¾ cup sour cream

- Preheat oven to 350°.

- Cream shortening, sugar and egg yolks in bowl. Add raisins, currants and nuts.

- Dissolve baking soda in 1 tablespoon hot water and add to mixture.

- Sift flour, ½ teaspoon salt, cloves, mace and cinnamon together and add alternately with sour cream to first mixture.

- Fold in 1 stiffly beaten egg white. (Use the other egg white in scrambled eggs or other dish.)

- Pour into 18 sprayed, floured muffin cups and bake for 15 to 20 minutes. Yields 18 cupcakes.

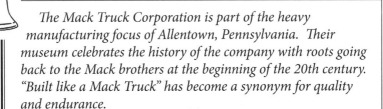

The Mack Truck Corporation is part of the heavy manufacturing focus of Allentown, Pennsylvania. Their museum celebrates the history of the company with roots going back to the Mack brothers at the beginning of the 20th century. "Built like a Mack Truck" has become a synonym for quality and endurance.

Whoopie Pies

This Pennsylvania Dutch dessert or snack has cake-like rounds on the top and bottom with a creamy, yummy filling between them. You may find them at grocery stores and convenience stores from Pennsylvania to Maine as a popular treat any time.

1 cup shortening, divided
1¼ cups sugar
2 eggs, separated
1 cup milk
2 teaspoons vanilla, divided
2 cups flour
¼ cup cocoa
1 teaspoon baking powder
1 teaspoon baking soda
2 cups powdered sugar, divided

- Preheat oven to 375°.

- Cream ½ cup shortening and sugar in large bowl. Beat egg yolks until lightly colored and pour into sugar mixture; add milk and 1 teaspoon vanilla. Mix well and beat again.

- In separate bowl, mix flour, cocoa, baking powder, baking soda and ½ teaspoon salt. Gradually pour a little flour mixture at a time into shortening-sugar mixture and beat after each addition.

- Drop spoonfuls of mixture onto unsprayed cookie sheets and bake for about 8 minutes or until done.

- Cream remaining ½ cup shortening, two-thirds of powdered sugar, 1 teaspoon vanilla and ½ teaspoon salt in large bowl.

- Beat egg whites until stiff. Pour remaining one-third of powdered sugar into egg whites and beat. Add shortening mixture to egg whites and beat for about 2 minutes.

- Make "sandwiches" of the cakes and filling. Wrap each individually and eat right away. Yields 8 to 12 pies.

Old-Fashioned Apple Pie

The best way to save time with this apple pie is to buy 1 (15 ounce) package refrigerated double piecrusts. Modern conveniences are good to have around.

Piecrust:

2 cups flour
⅔ cup shortening

- Combine flour and 1 teaspoon salt in large bowl. Add shortening a little at a time and stir until lumps are small.

- Slowly pour in 3 tablespoons cold water and stir until it mixes well. Divide dough into 2 pieces and place on floured, countertop.

- Roll out each half of dough to about ⅛-inch thick. Place 1 inside 9-inch pie pan. Save remaining half for upper crust.

Pie Filling:

2 tablespoons lemon juice
6 cups peeled, cored, sliced Gala apples
1 cup plus 1 tablespoon sugar
2 tablespoons flour
1½ teaspoons ground cinnamon

- Preheat oven to 400°.

- Sprinkle lemon juice over apples and stir to mix with all slices in bowl.

- In separate bowl, mix sugar, flour and cinnamon. Pour over apples and stir well.

- Pour pie filling into piecrust. Place second piecrust over top and seal edges of piecrusts. Cut slits in top piecrust. Bake for 60 minutes and cool before serving. Serves 8.

Apple Butter-Pumpkin Pie

1 cup canned pumpkin
1 cup apple butter
¾ cup packed brown sugar
½ teaspoon ground cinnamon
½ teaspoon ground nutmeg
3 eggs, slight beaten
1 (5 ounce) can evaporated milk
⅓ cup milk
1 (9 inch) unbaked piecrust
Whipped topping, thawed, or ice cream

- Preheat oven to 350°.

- Combine pumpkin, apple butter, brown sugar, cinnamon, nutmeg and ½ teaspoon salt until it blends well. Stir in eggs, evaporated milk and milk; blend thoroughly.

- Pour mixture into piecrust. Cover edges of crust with foil so they will not over-brown. Bake for 45 to 50 minutes until a knife inserted in the center comes out clean.

- Cool pie and serve with whipped topping or ice cream. Serves 6 to 8.

Valley Forge was where American soldiers spent the winter of 1777-1778 in great privation, lacking food and shelter and subject to disease. "To see men without clothes to cover their nakedness, without blankets to lie upon, without shoes ... without a house or hut to cover them until those could be built, and submitting without a murmur, is a proof of patience and obedience which, in my opinion, can scarcely be paralleled." (George Washington at Valley Forge, April 21, 1778). Today Valley Forge is a National Historical Park.

Creamy Blackberry Pie

4 cups fresh blackberries
1 (9 inch) refrigerated piecrust
1 cup sugar
⅓ cup flour
2 eggs, beaten
½ cup sour cream

- Preheat oven to 350°.

- Place blackberries in piecrust. Combine sugar and flour in bowl.

- In separate bowl, blend eggs and sour cream and add sugar-flour mixture to eggs. Spoon over blackberries.

Topping:

½ cup sugar
½ cup flour
¼ cup (½ stick) butter

- Combine sugar, flour and butter in bowl. Mix well. Crumble evenly over sour cream mixture. Bake for 1 hour or until light brown. Serves 8.

Old-Time Pineapple-Chess Pie

1½ cups sugar
1 tablespoon cornmeal
2 tablespoons flour
6 tablespoons (¾ stick) butter, melted
2 eggs, beaten
1 (8 ounce) can crushed pineapple
1 (9 inch) refrigerated piecrust

- Preheat oven to 350°.

- Combine sugar, cornmeal, flour and pinch of salt in bowl and mix. Stir in butter, eggs and pineapple and beat.

- Pour into piecrust and bake for 45 minutes. Serves 8.

Birthday Pumpkin Chiffon Pie

The best pumpkin pie you'll ever eat!

1 (1 ounce) packet unflavored gelatin
2 eggs
1¼ cups sugar
1¼ cups canned pumpkin
⅔ cup milk
½ teaspoon ground ginger
½ teaspoon ground nutmeg
½ teaspoon ground cinnamon
1 (8 ounce) carton whipping cream
1 (9 inch) baked piecrust

- Soften gelatin in ¼ cup cold water in bowl and set aside.

- In separate bowl, beat eggs for 3 minutes. Add sugar, pumpkin, milk, ginger, nutmeg, cinnamon and ½ teaspoon salt and mix well.

- Pour mixture into double boiler and stir constantly until mixture reaches custard consistency (coats the back of a metal spoon). Mix in softened gelatin and dissolve in hot pumpkin mixture; cool.

- When mixture is cool, whip cream in bowl until very stiff and fold into pumpkin mixture. (Do not use whipped topping.) Pour into piecrust and refrigerate for several hours before slicing. Serves 8.

TIP: *Original "chiffon" pies had egg whites whipped and folded into pie. Because raw eggs are not good in uncooked recipes, this recipe cooks the whole eggs and adds whipped cream. It is delicious!*

> *King Charles II of England granted a vast tract of land to William Penn in 1681 to offset a large debt owed to Penn's father. This grant included modern-day Pennsylvania and parts of other states. In return for the grant, Penn was required to send two beaver pelts to the king annually.*

Farmhouse Buttermilk Pie

4 eggs
1 cup sugar
3 tablespoons flour
2 tablespoons butter, melted
3 tablespoons lemon juice
1¼ cups buttermilk*
½ teaspoon lemon extract
1 (9 inch) baked piecrust, chilled

- Preheat oven to 350°.

- Beat eggs in large bowl until light and fluffy. Gradually add sugar and blend in flour, butter and lemon juice. Add buttermilk slowly and mix until it blends well. Stir in lemon extract.

- Pour into piecrust; bake for 45 minutes or until knife inserted in center come out clean.

- Serve room temperature or chilled, but refrigerate any leftovers. Serves 8.

TIP: To make buttermilk, mix 1 cup milk with 1 tablespoon lemon juice or vinegar and let stand for about 10 minutes.

Enjoy a week's worth of summer fun and exhibits at the Bedford County Fair in Bedford, Pennsylvania. From a baked goods auction to competitions in fruits, vegetables and other crops to livestock and farm equipment contests and exhibitions, it's a traditional county fair with activities for the entire family.

German Chocolate Pie

1 (4 ounce) package German sweet chocolate
½ cup (1 stick) butter
1 (12 ounce) can evaporated milk
1½ cups sugar
3 tablespoons cornstarch
2 eggs
1 teaspoon vanilla
1 (9 inch) refrigerated piecrust
1 (3.5 ounce) can flaked coconut
½ cup chopped pecans

- Preheat oven to 350°.

- Melt chocolate with butter in saucepan over low heat and gradually blend in evaporated milk.

- Combine sugar, cornstarch and ⅛ teaspoon salt in bowl and mix thoroughly. Beat in eggs and vanilla, gradually blend into chocolate mixture and pour into piecrust.

- Combine coconut and pecans in bowl and sprinkle over filling.

- Bake for 45 to 50 minutes. Filling will be soft but will set while cooking.

- Cool for at least 4 hours before slicing. Serves 8.

Hershey, Pennsylvania is the Chocolate Capital of the United States. Not only does it feature the world's largest chocolate factory, Hershey includes great leisure destinations such as Hershey's Chocolate World, dedicated to food, shops, entertainment and everything chocolate and Hersheypark, a major amusement park with more than 60 rides and attractions.

Famous Shoo-Fly Pie

1 cup flour
½ cup packed brown sugar
1 teaspoon baking soda
Shortening
½ cup molasses
1 (9 inch) frozen piecrust, unbaked

- Preheat oven to 350°.

- Mix flour, brown sugar, baking soda and a pinch of salt in bowl. Add just enough shortening to make mixture crumbly.

- Mix molasses and ½ cup boiling water in saucepan. While hot, pour into piecrust. Spread crust crumbles over top of molasses.

- Bake until firm in middle and toothpick inserted in center comes out clean. Serves 8.

Easy Cinnamon-Apple Cobbler

2 (20 ounce) cans apple pie filling
½ cup packed brown sugar
1½ teaspoons ground cinnamon
1 (18 ounce) box yellow cake mix
½ cup (1 stick) butter, melted

- Preheat oven to 350°.

- Spread apple pie filling in sprayed, floured 9 x 13-inch baking dish.

- Sprinkle with brown sugar and cinnamon and top with dry cake mix. Drizzle melted butter over top of cake mix.

- Bake for 50 minutes or until light brown and bubbly. Serves 16.

Simple Apple Crisp

Peeling apples is the most difficult part of this recipe.

5 cups peeled, cored, sliced apples
½ cup (1 stick) butter, melted
1 cup quick-cooking oats
½ cup firmly packed brown sugar
⅓ cup flour

- Preheat over to 375°.

- Place apple slices in sprayed, floured 8-inch or 9-inch square baking pan.

- Combine butter, oats, brown sugar and flour in bowl and sprinkle mixture over apples.

- Bake for 40 to 45 minutes or until apples are tender and topping is golden brown. Serves 9.

TIP: For a change, add 1 teaspoon cinnamon and ½ cup raisins or dried cranberries to apples before sprinkling with topping.

Andrew Carnegie (1835-1919) was one of the most prominent industrialists of the 19th century. He was born in Scotland and his family emigrated to Pittsburgh, Pennsylvania when he was 13. He began working in a textile mill for $1.20 per week. He founded Carnegie Steel Company which became the largest and most profitable industrial enterprise in the world. He retired and spent his last 18 years spending his money on great philanthropic projects, funding more than 3,000 libraries in 47 states and in the United Kingdom, Canada, Ireland, Australia, New Zealand, the West Indies and Fiji. He also made large donations to scientific research and efforts for world peace. He donated $2 million to found the Carnegie Institute of Technology at Pittsburgh which is now part of Carnegie Mellon University. At the time of his death, he had given away more than $350 million (a sum of $4.3 billion adjusted to 2005 dollars).

Blueberry Crumble

Great crumbles. Great flavors.

1 (13 ounce) box wild blueberry muffin mix
⅓ cup plus ¼ cup sugar, divided
1½ teaspoon ground cinnamon, divided
¼ cup (½ stick) butter, melted
⅔ cup chopped pecans
1 (20 ounce) can blueberry pie filling
Vanilla ice cream

- Preheat oven to 350°.

- Combine muffin mix, ⅓ cup sugar, ½ teaspoon cinnamon and butter in bowl and mix until crumbly (do not add blueberries in muffin mix). Add pecans and set aside.

- Pour blueberry pie filling into sprayed, floured 7 x 11-inch glass baking dish.

- Drain canned blueberries from muffin mix and pour over top of pie filling.

- Sprinkle ¼ cup sugar mixed with 1 teaspoon cinnamon over top; then, with your hands, crumble muffin mixture over top of pie filling.

- Bake for 35 minutes. To serve, hot or at room temperature, top with a dip of vanilla ice cream. Serves 8.

Pennsylvania ranks fourth in the nation in milk production and the manufacture of ice cream. Dairy farming is the largest segment of Pennsylvania's agricultural industry.

Terrific Blueberry Streusel-Cobbler

1 (14 ounce) package frozen blueberries, thawed
1 (14 ounce) can sweetened condensed milk
2 teaspoons grated lemon peel
¾ cup (1½ sticks) plus 2 tablespoons butter, softened
2 cups biscuit mix, divided
⅔ cup packed brown sugar
¾ cup chopped pecans

- Preheat oven to 325°.

- Combine blueberries, sweetened condensed milk and lemon peel in bowl.

- In separate bowl, cut ¾ cup butter into 1½ cups biscuit mix and stir until crumbly. Add blueberry mixture and spread in sprayed, floured 9 x 13-inch baking dish.

- Combine remaining biscuit mix and brown sugar in bowl. Cut in 2 tablespoons butter until crumbly, add pecans and sprinkle over cobbler.

- Bake for 55 to 60 minutes or until toothpick inserted in center comes out clean.

Blueberry Sauce:

½ cup sugar
1 tablespoon cornstarch
½ teaspoon ground cinnamon
¼ teaspoon ground nutmeg
1 (14 ounce) package frozen blueberries, thawed
Vanilla ice cream

- Combine sugar, cornstarch, cinnamon and nutmeg in small saucepan and gradually add ½ cup water. Cook and stir until it thickens. Stir in blueberries.

- Serve square of cobbler with ice cream on top and pour blueberry sauce over all. Serves 10.

Easy Cherry Cobbler

2 (20 ounce) cans cherry pie filling
1 (18 ounce) box white cake mix
¾ cup (1½ sticks) butter, melted
1 (4 ounce) package slivered almonds
Whipped topping, thawed

- Preheat oven to 350°.

- Spread pie filling in sprayed, floured 9 x 13-inch baking pan. Sprinkle cake mix over pie filling.

- Drizzle butter over top and sprinkle with almonds. Bake for 45 minutes. Top with whipped topping to serve. Serves 16.

Perfect Peach Cobbler

3 cups sliced fresh or canned peaches
1 tablespoon lemon juice
1 cup flour
1 cup sugar
1 egg, beaten
6 tablespoons (¾ stick) butter, melted

- Preheat oven to 375°.

- Place peach slices in sprayed, floured 7 x 11-inch baking dish and sprinkle with lemon juice.

- In separate bowl, mix flour and sugar; add egg and stir until mixture is crumbly.

- Scatter crumbly dough over peach slices and drizzle butter on top.

- Bake for about 35 minutes. Serves 4.

The average farm in Pennsylvania covers 133 acres. Only 4% of farms have more than 500 acres.

Traditional Cherry Custard Pie

1 (15 ounce) package refrigerated piecrusts (only 1 is used)
1 (16 ounce) can sour cherries, drained
2 cups milk
3 eggs, beaten
1 teaspoon vanilla
½ cup sugar
2 tablespoons flour

- Preheat oven to 400°.

- Place piecrust in 9-inch pie pan. Place drained cherries in piecrust and spread evenly over crust.

- Heat milk just to the boiling point in saucepan, but do not boil or let milk scorch in bottom of pan. Add eggs and vanilla and mix well.

- Mix sugar and flour in bowl and pour into milk mixture. Beat mixture well and pour over cherries in piecrust.

- Bake for 35 to 40 minutes or until pie sets in center and is firm. Serves 8.

Robert Morris (1734-1806) was a signer of the Declaration of Independence. Born in England, he arrived in America in 1744. A wealthy businessman, he was elected to the Continental Congress in 1775 and served as a delegate to the Constitutional Convention and as a U.S. Senator. Almost single-handedly, he supervised the financing of the Revolutionary War and the founding of the Bank of the United States.

Flashy Almond-Fudge Shortbread

1 cup (2 sticks) butter, softened
1 cup powdered sugar
1¼ cups flour
1 (12 ounce) package chocolate chips
1 (14 ounce) can sweetened condensed milk
½ teaspoon almond extract
1 (2.5 ounce) package chopped almonds, toasted

- Preheat oven to 350°.

- Beat butter, powdered sugar and ¼ teaspoon salt in bowl and stir in flour.

- Pat into sprayed, floured 9 x 13-inch baking pan and bake for 15 minutes.

- Melt chocolate chips with sweetened condensed milk in medium saucepan over low heat and stir until chips melt. Stir in almond extract.

- Spread evenly over shortbread and sprinkle with almonds.

- Refrigerate for several hours or until firm and cut into bars. They may be stored at room temperature. Yields 2 dozen bars.

The Wilbur Chocolate Company in Lititz, Pennsylvania was founded in 1865. It produces more than 150 million pounds of chocolate annually.

Easy Angel Macaroons

1 (16 ounce) package 1-step angel food cake mix
1½ teaspoons almond extract
2 cups flaked coconut

- Preheat oven to 350°.

- Beat cake mix, ½ cup water and almond extract in bowl for 30 seconds.

- Scrape bowl and beat on medium speed for 1 minute. Fold in coconut.

- Drop rounded teaspoonfuls of dough onto parchment paper-lined cookie sheet and bake for 10 to 12 minutes or until cookies set.

- Remove parchment paper with cookies to wire rack to cool. Yields 3 dozen cookies.

Classic Date Log Cookies

1 cup dates
¼ cup sugar
1 (3 ounce) package cream cheese, softened
½ cup (1 stick) butter
1 cup flour
Powdered sugar

- Preheat oven to 275°.

- Cook dates and sugar in ¼ cup water in saucepan over medium heat until a smooth paste forms.

- Beat cream cheese and butter in bowl until smooth. Add flour and a little salt and mix well.

- On lightly floured wax paper, roll out dough and cut in 3-inch squares.

- Place 1 teaspoon date mixture on each square and roll into logs. Seal ends with fork.

- Bake for 20 minutes. Roll in powdered sugar and serve. Yields 2 dozen cookies.

Applesauce Yummies

4 cups flour
2 teaspoons baking soda
1 teaspoon ground cinnamon
1 teaspoon ground nutmeg
½ teaspoon ground allspice
1 cup (2 sticks) butter, softened
1½ cups sugar
1½ cups packed brown sugar
3 eggs, beaten
2 cups applesauce
1 cup golden raisins
1½ cups chopped walnuts

- Preheat oven to 400°.

- Combine flour, baking soda, 1 teaspoon salt, cinnamon, nutmeg and allspice in bowl.

- In separate bowl, combine butter, sugar and brown sugar; beat until fluffy. Stir in eggs and applesauce.

- Add dry ingredients and mix well. Stir in raisins and walnuts.

- Drop teaspoonfuls of dough onto sprayed cookie sheet and bake for 8 to 10 minutes or just until cookies brown lightly. Yields 5 dozen cookies.

The first capital of Pennsylvania was Philadelphia in the colonial period. The first permanent meeting place for the colonial legislature, however, was not established until 1729 when the legislature selected the structure now known as Independence Hall. Lancaster replaced Philadelphia as the capital in 1799; meetings were held in the Lancaster courthouse. In 1812 Harrisburg was selected as the capital. The first Capitol was built there in 1822.

Classic Gingersnaps

¾ cup packed brown sugar
¾ cup butter or shortening
¾ cup light molasses
1 egg
¾ cup flour
2 teaspoons baking soda
1 teaspoon ground cinnamon
1 teaspoon ground ginger
½ teaspoon ground cloves
¼ cup sugar

- Mix brown sugar and butter or shortening in bowl until smooth and creamy. Pour molasses and egg into mixture and beat well.

- In separate bowl, combine flour, baking soda, cinnamon, ginger, cloves and ¼ teaspoon salt. Gradually add to butter mixture and stir after each addition. Mix well.

- Refrigerate overnight or for several hours.

- When ready to bake, preheat oven to 350°.

- Form dough in 1 to 2-inch balls and roll in sugar. Place 2 inches apart on sprayed cookie sheet. Bake for 10 to 12 minutes. Yields 3 dozen cookies.

In the 1700's, the Conestoga wagon was invented by German farmers in Pennsylvania's Conestoga Valley. The wagon was developed with better steering and braking capacities and was important to the westward expansion of the United States in the 1700's and 1800's.

Hugs and Kisses Molasses Cookies

1 cup butter, softened
1½ cups sugar
1 egg
¾ cup molasses
3 cups flour
1 teaspoon baking powder
1 teaspoon ground ginger
1 cup chopped nuts

- Cream butter and sugar in large bowl. Add egg and molasses and continue to cream mixture.

- In separate bowl, mix flour, baking powder and ginger and add a little at a time to creamed mixture. Add nuts and mix well.

- Form into 3 rolls, wrap in plastic wrap and refrigerate overnight.

- When ready to bake, preheat oven to 350°.

- Cut rolls into ¼-inch slices and bake for about 10 minutes or until light brown. Yields 4 dozen cookies.

Andrew W. Mellon (1855-1937) was born in Pittsburgh, Pennsylvania. He served as the 49th Secretary of the Treasury (1921-1932), the only one to serve under three presidents (Harding, Coolidge and Hoover). As secretary, he reformed the tax system and reduced the national debt. In 1913, Mellon and his brother founded the Mellon Institute of Industrial Research as a memorial to their father. It is today a part of Carnegie Mellon University.

Grammy's Ginger-Oat Cookies

½ cup (1 stick) butter, softened
¾ cup sugar
¾ cup packed brown sugar
1 egg
½ teaspoon vanilla
1 cup flour
½ teaspoon baking soda
½ cup finely chopped crystallized ginger
1½ cups quick-cooking oats
1 (6 ounce) package chocolate chips
½ cup chopped pecans

- Preheat oven to 350°.

- Combine butter, sugar, brown sugar, egg, 1 tablespoon water and vanilla in bowl and beat.

- Add flour, baking soda and ginger and mix well.

- Add oats, chocolate chips and pecans and mix well.

- Drop teaspoonfuls of dough onto sprayed cookie sheet and bake for 12 to 15 minutes or until cookies are light brown. Yields 4 dozen cookies.

Lebanon, Pennsylvania is the home of the Lebanon Area Fair. Held in the summer for more than 50 years, it takes nine days to cover all its events and competitions from livestock judging to kids' activities.

Hurly-Burly Oatmeal Cookies

1 cup packed brown sugar
1 cup sugar
1 cup shortening
2 eggs
2 teaspoons vanilla
1 teaspoon baking soda
1½ cups flour
3 cups quick-cooking oats
1 cup chopped pecans

- Preheat oven to 350°.

- Combine brown sugar, sugar, shortening, eggs, 2 tablespoons water and vanilla in bowl and beat well.

- Add 1 teaspoon salt, baking soda and flour and mix well. Add oats and pecans and mix well.

- Drop teaspoonfuls of dough onto sprayed cookie sheet and bake for 14 to 15 minutes or until cookies brown. Yields 4 dozen cookies.

Dickens of a Christmas in Wellsboro, Pennsylvania attracts 30,000 visitors each year in early December. Step back into the Victorian era for a weekend featuring a marketplace filled with food and gifts. There are strolling singers, musicians and other entertainers – all in Victorian costumes.

Young Whippersnappers

¾ cup packed brown sugar
¾ cup sugar
1½ cups shortening
2 large eggs
1½ cups flour
½ teaspoon baking soda
2¾ cups oats
½ cup chopped pecans
½ cup peanut butter
1½ teaspoons vanilla
1 (6 ounce) package chocolate chips

- Preheat over to 350°.

- Cream brown sugar, sugar and shortening in bowl. Add eggs and beat.

- In separate bowl, sift flour, baking soda and ½ teaspoon salt and add to sugar mixture.

- Stir in oats, pecans, peanut butter, vanilla and chocolate chips.

- Drop teaspoonfuls of dough onto sprayed cookie sheet and bake for 12 to 14 minutes or until edges of cookies begin to brown. Yields 4 dozen cookies.

Allentown, Pennsylvania's third largest city, has the unique distinction of being home to the Liberty Bell in 1777-1778 during the British occupation of Philadelphia. The bell was spirited away from Philadelphia for fear of its being melted down to make a British cannon and it was hidden in the basement of the Old Zion Reformed Church which still stands today with a monument to this event.

Just Butter Cookies

1 cup (2 sticks) butter, softened
1 (1 pound) box powdered sugar
1 egg
1 teaspoon almond extract
1 teaspoon vanilla
2½ cups plus 1 tablespoon flour
¾ teaspoon cream of tartar
1 teaspoon baking soda
Sugar

- Cream butter, powdered sugar, egg, almond extract and vanilla in bowl and mix well.

- In separate bowl, sift flour, cream of tartar and baking soda and add to creamed mixture. Cover and refrigerate for several hours.

- When ready to bake, preheat oven to 350°.

- Roll cookie dough into ¼-inch thickness and use cookie cutters to make desired shapes. Place on sprayed cookie sheet.

- Bake for 7 to 8 minutes, but do not brown.

- Sprinkle a little sugar over each cookie while still hot.
  Yields 2 dozen cookies.

Philadelphia was the first capital and the largest city in the U.S. in the 18th century. It was here that the Continental Congress met and approved the Declaration of Independence and that the Constitutional Convention was held.

Mmm-Mmm Sugar Cookies

½ cup (1 stick) butter, softened
1 cup sugar
1 egg
1 tablespoon cream
½ teaspoon vanilla
2 cups flour
1 teaspoon baking powder

- Preheat oven to 375°.

- Cream butter in bowl and slowly add sugar. Beat until light and fluffy.

- In separate bowl, combine egg, cream and vanilla; add to butter mixture and beat to mix.

- In a separate bowl, combine flour, baking powder and ¼ teaspoon salt. Add flour mixture to butter mixture a little at a time and mix after each addition.

- Drop teaspoonfuls of mixture onto sprayed cookie sheet.

- Bake for about 8 to 10 minutes. Yields about 5 dozen cookies.

The Pittsburgh Folk Festival, held annually in May for more than 50 years, celebrates the city's ethnic diversity with live music, arts and crafts, ethnic food and much more. Over 30 national origins are represented with traditional dance, cultural exhibits and shopping in an international bazaar.

Yankee Doodle's Snickerdoodles

½ cup (1 stick) butter, softened
½ cup shortening
1¾ cups sugar, divided
2 eggs
2¼ cups flour
2 teaspoons cream of tartar
1 teaspoon baking soda
2 teaspoons ground cinnamon

- Preheat oven to 350°.

- Mix butter, shortening, 1½ cups sugar and eggs in medium bowl and beat well.

- Stir in flour, cream of tartar, baking soda and ¼ teaspoon salt.

- Shape dough by rounded teaspoonfuls into balls.

- Mix remaining ¼ cup sugar and cinnamon in small bowl and roll balls in mixture to cover.

- Place balls 2 inches apart on unsprayed cookie sheet and use bottom of jar or glass to mash cookies flat.

- Bake 8 to 10 minutes or until edges just begin to brown. Yields 24 to 30 cookies.

Each year on Christmas Day Washington's "Crossing of the Delaware" is reenacted at Washington Crossing Historic Park. This celebrates a key victory by General George Washington in defeating the Hessian troops in Trenton, New Jersey by crossing the Delaware River from Pennsylvania to New Jersey under cover of darkness on December 25, 1776.

Classic Shortbread Cookies

2 cups (4 sticks) butter, softened
1 cup powdered sugar
4 cups flour
Additional powdered sugar

- Cream butter in bowl until light and fluffy. Gradually add powdered sugar and beat vigorously after each addition until sugar completely dissolves.

- Add flour, a little at a time, and beat well after each addition. Refrigerate dough for 1 hour.

- When ready to bake, preheat oven to 350°.

- Sprinkle surface with equal parts of flour and powdered sugar and turn one-third of dough at a time onto surface.

- Pat into ½-inch thickness and cut cookies with 1½-inch biscuit cutter.

- Place on unsprayed cookie sheet and prick tops of cookies with fork to make a criss-cross design.

- Bake for 15 to 20 minutes or until light golden color.

- Remove from oven and cool slightly before lightly dusting with powdered sugar. Yields 4 dozen cookies.

Bubble gum was invented by Walter Dierner in 1928 in Philadelphia. In the first year of production, the value of the new gum sold was over $1.5 million.

Mom's Sand Tarts

1 cup (2 sticks) butter, softened
1 teaspoon vanilla
6 tablespoons powdered sugar
2 cups flour
1 cup chopped pecans
Powdered sugar

- Preheat oven to 350°.

- Cream butter, vanilla and powdered sugar in large bowl. Gradually add flour a little at a time and mix well. Add pecans and mix well.

- Form half-moon shapes on sprayed cookie sheet and bake for 5 to 8 minutes or until light brown. Cool and dredge in powdered sugar on both sides. Yields 3 dozen cookies.

Holiday Spritz Cookies

½ cup plus 2 tablespoons (1¼ sticks) butter, softened
1¼ cups sugar
1 egg, well beaten
1 teaspoon almond flavoring
Food coloring
3 cups flour
1 teaspoon baking powder

- Preheat oven to 350°. Cream butter and sugar in bowl.

- Add egg and almond flavoring and beat well. Add food coloring of your choice to add a holiday touch. Stir flour and baking powder into creamed mixture.

- Using cookie press, press dough in desired shapes on unsprayed cookie sheet. Bake for about 8 minutes or until cookies are light brown. Yields 3 dozen cookies.

TIP: *Use some of the decorative icings or sprinkles found in grocery store to decorate cookies.*

Tangy Orange Balls

1 (12 ounce) box vanilla wafers, crushed
½ cup (1 stick) butter, melted
1 (16 ounce) box powdered sugar
1 (6 ounce) can frozen orange juice concentrate, thawed
1 cup finely chopped pecans

- Combine vanilla wafers, butter, powdered sugar and orange juice concentrate in bowl and mix well.

- Roll into balls and roll in chopped pecans. Store in airtight container. Yields 1½ dozen balls.

Butter-Pecan Turtle Bars

2 cups flour
1½ cups packed light brown sugar, divided
¾ cup (1½ sticks) plus ⅔ cup (1⅓ sticks) butter, divided
1½ cups coarsely chopped pecans
4 (1 ounce) squares semi-sweet chocolate

- Preheat oven to 350°.

- Combine flour, ¾ cup brown sugar and ½ cup butter in bowl and blend until crumbly.

- Pat down crust mixture evenly in sprayed, floured 9 x 13-inch baking pan. Sprinkle pecans over crust and set aside.

- Combine remaining brown sugar and ⅔ cup butter in small saucepan. Cook over medium heat and stir constantly. Bring mixture to a boil for 1 minute and stir constantly.

- Drizzle caramel sauce over pecans and crust and bake for 18 to 20 minutes or until caramel layer is bubbly. Remove from oven and cool.

- Melt chocolate squares and ¼ cup butter in saucepan and stir until smooth. Pour over bars and spread around. Cool and cut into bars. Yields 12 bars.

Very Chocolate Streusel Bars

1¾ cups flour
1½ cups powdered sugar
½ cup cocoa
1 cup (2 sticks) butter, softened
1 (8 ounce) package cream cheese, softened
1 (14 ounce) can sweetened condensed milk
1 egg
2 teaspoons vanilla
½ cup chopped pecans

- Preheat oven to 350°.

- Combine flour, powdered sugar and cocoa in large bowl. Cut in butter until crumbly.

- Set aside 1 cup crumb mixture and press remaining dough firmly in sprayed, floured 9 x 13-inch baking pan.

- Bake for 15 minutes.

- Beat cream cheese in large bowl until fluffy. Gradually beat in sweetened condensed milk until smooth.

- Add egg and vanilla and mix well. Pour over prepared crust.

- Combine pecans with reserved crumb mixture and sprinkle over cream cheese mixture.

- Bake for 25 minutes or until bubbly.

- Cool and refrigerate. Cut into bars and store in covered container. Yields 12 to 14 bars.

Pennsylvania has more than 200 covered bridges, more than any other state in the U.S.

Crunchy Peanut Brittle

2 cups sugar
½ cup light corn syrup
2 cups dry-roasted peanuts
1 tablespoon butter
1 teaspoon baking soda

- Combine sugar and corn syrup in saucepan. Cook over low heat and stir constantly until sugar dissolves. Cover and cook over medium heat for additional 2 minutes.

- Add peanuts and cook uncovered, stirring occasionally, to hard-crack stage (300°). Stir in butter and baking soda and *quickly* pour into sprayed jellyroll pan and spread thinly.

- Cool and break into pieces. Yields 3 dozen pieces.

Sugar Plum Candy

1¼ pounds almond bark, chopped
1½ cups red and green miniature marshmallows
1½ cups peanut butter cereal
1½ cups rice crispy cereal
1½ cups mixed nuts

- Melt almond bark in double boiler over low heat.

- Place marshmallows, cereals and nuts in large bowl.

- Pour melted bark over mixture and stir to coat.

- Drop teaspoonfuls of mixture onto wax paper-lined cookie sheet.

- Let stand until set and store in airtight container. Yields 3 dozen.

Fun White Chocolate Fudge

1 (8 ounce) package cream cheese, softened
4 cups powdered sugar
1½ teaspoons vanilla
12 ounces almond bark, melted
¾ cup chopped pecans

- Beat cream cheese in bowl on medium speed until smooth, gradually add powdered sugar and vanilla and beat well to mix. Stir in melted almond bark and pecans.

- Spread into sprayed 8-inch square pan. Refrigerate until firm. Yields 12 squares.

Date-Nut Loaf Candy

6 cups sugar
1 (12 ounce) can evaporated milk
½ cup light corn syrup
1 cup (2 sticks) butter
2 (8 ounce) boxes chopped dates
3 cups chopped pecans or walnuts
1 tablespoon vanilla

- Cook sugar, evaporated milk, corn syrup and butter in saucepan for 5 minutes or until it boils. Stir constantly with wooden or plastic spoon so mixture will not scorch.

- Add dates and cook until it forms soft-ball stage in cup of cold water (234°). Remove from heat and beat until thick. Add pecans and vanilla and stir until very thick.

- Spoon out mixture onto damp cup towel to make roll. Keep wrapped until it is firm enough to slice. Yields 2 rolls.

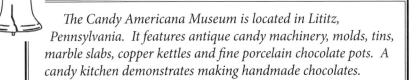

The Candy Americana Museum is located in Lititz, Pennsylvania. It features antique candy machinery, molds, tins, marble slabs, copper kettles and fine porcelain chocolate pots. A candy kitchen demonstrates making handmade chocolates.

Apple Dumplings

1½ cups packed brown sugar, divided
¼ cup chopped pecans
2 tablespoons butter, softened
6 baking apples, cored
1 (15 ounce/2 piecrusts) package refrigerated piecrusts

- Preheat oven to 400°.

- Mix ½ cup brown sugar, pecans and butter in bowl and spoon mixture into each apple.

- Roll both piecrusts to ⅛-inch thickness. Cut into 6 squares approximately 7 inches each.

- Wrap 1 square around each apple, pinch edges to seal and place in baking dish.

- Place remaining 1 cup brown sugar and ½ cup water in saucepan over medium heat and stir until sugar dissolves. Pour syrup over dumplings.

- Bake for 30 to 35 minutes or until tender and baste occasionally with syrup. Serves 6.

TIP: *For even more flavorful dumplings, add 2 teaspoons ground cinnamon or apple pie spice with brown sugar, pecans and butter.*

Usually celebrated in September, the annual Pennsylvania Bavarian Oktoberfest in Canonsburg, Pennsylvania is based on the celebrated German festivals with great foods and beverages, fun activities for children and more. It's one of the top 10 Oktoberfests in the country.

Oma's Bread Pudding

1½ cups breadcrumbs
3 cups hot milk
2 eggs, beaten
⅔ cup sugar
1 tablespoon butter
½ teaspoon vanilla
½ cup chopped nuts
Whipped cream

- Preheat oven to 350°.

- Combine breadcrumbs, milk, eggs, sugar, butter and ¼ teaspoon salt in bowl. Mix well.

- Add vanilla and nuts. Turn mixture into 7 x 11-inch sprayed baking dish.

- Bake for 35 to 40 minutes or until firm. Serve with whipped cream. Serves 6.

Home-Style Sweet Rice

1 cup rice
1 (12 ounce) can evaporated milk
¾ cup sugar
Ground cinnamon

- Cover rice with water in saucepan, add a pinch of salt and cook until rice is almost tender. (Add water if needed.)

- Add evaporated milk and sugar and cook until rice is tender.

- Pour into baking dish and serve. Sprinkle with additional sugar and a little cinnamon to taste. Serves 4.

The banana split was invented by David Strickler in Latrobe, Pennsylvania in 1904. The original price was 10 cents.

Orange Bavarian Cream

1½ cups vanilla wafer crumbs (about 34 wafers), divided
2 (6 ounce) cartons orange yogurt
1 (3.5 ounce) package vanilla instant pudding mix
¼ cup powdered sugar
1 (8 ounce) carton whipped topping, thawed
½ teaspoon orange flavoring
3 (11 ounce) cans mandarin oranges, drained   , divided

- Crush vanilla wafers in food processor or crush in resealable plastic bag.

- Beat yogurt and pudding mix in bowl for 30 seconds. Fold in powdered sugar, whipped topping and orange flavoring.

- Layer mixture in 8 parfait glasses with oranges and crushed vanilla wafers. Save enough orange slices and crumbs to top each serving. Serves 8.

Ice Cream with Hot Raspberry Sauce

2 pints fresh raspberries
¾ cup sugar
2 tablespoons cornstarch
Ice cream

- Soak raspberries with sugar in ½ cup water in saucepan for about 20 minutes. Pour small amount of water from raspberries into small cup. Add cornstarch and stir well to dissolve cornstarch and any lumps.

- Pour raspberries and cornstarch mixture into blender and process to desired consistency. Pour processed raspberries into strainer over saucepan.

- Bring to a boil, reduce heat to low and cook for 2 to 4 minutes or until sauce thickens; stir constantly. Serve over ice cream. Serves 4.

Opa's Old-Fashioned Ice Cream

4 large eggs, separated
2 tablespoons flour
2¾ cups sugar
1 tablespoon vanilla
3 quarts milk, divided
1 (1 pint) carton whipping cream
Rock salt

- Beat egg yolks in bowl until light and fluffy.

- In separate bowl, combine flour, sugar and vanilla; add to egg yolks with 1 quart milk and beat well.

- Beat egg whites until stiff and fold into yolk-milk mixture. Pour into double boiler and heat, stirring constantly, until mixture thickens. Pour into 1-gallon ice cream freezer.

- Add whipping cream and enough milk to reach 3 inches from top of freezer.

- Cover tightly and pack freezer with ice and rock salt and freeze according to manufacturer's directions. Serves 10 to 14.

TIP: *To make peach or banana ice cream, add 2 cups diced fruit before adding remaining milk.*

Pennsylvania is the home of the third largest group of Amish in the U.S., after Ohio and Indiana. Their farms, located in the Lancaster County area, are among the nation's most productive.

Black Cherry-Chocolate Frozen Yogurt

1½ cups pitted black cherries, fresh or frozen, divided
2 (8 ounce) containers cherry yogurt
½ cup honey
½ teaspoon almond extract
1 square (1 ounce) square semisweet chocolate, chopped

- Coarsely chop ½ cup cherries and set aside.

- In a food processor or blender, combine remaining cherries, yogurt, honey and almond extract; blend until smooth. Stir in set aside cherries and transfer mixture to ice cream freezer and freeze according to manufacturer's directions.

- Combine chocolate with 2 tablespoons water in small saucepan and stir over low heat until chocolate melts and mixture is smooth. Set aside to cool.

- When yogurt is frozen, divide evenly between 6 sherbet dishes and top with chocolate. Serves 6.

Founder of Hershey's Chocolate, Milton S. Hershey (1857-1945), was born on a farm near Derry Church, Pennsylvania. In 1883, he began the Lancaster Caramel Company. After seeing German chocolate-making equipment at the World's Columbian Exposition in 1893 in Chicago, Hershey bought the technology and began producing a variety of chocolate candies. At this time, milk chocolate was a luxury product of Switzerland and the trade secrets were not available. But Milton Hershey developed his own recipe for milk chocolate and marketed his products at an affordable price. In 1905, he completed the world's largest chocolate factory designed with the latest advancements in mass production.

Bibliography

Agriculture in Pennsylvania   phmc.state.pa.us.

Backroads of Pennsylvania (Pictorial Discovery Guide); Marcus Schneck; Voyageur Press; 2003.

Moore Handbooks Pennsylvania; Joanne Miller; Avalon Travel Publishing; 2005.

Pennsylvania   www.50states.com

Pennsylvania   www. en.wikipedia.org

Pennsylvania: A History of the Commonwealth; Randall Miller; Pennsylvania State University Press; 2002.

Pennsylvania Agriculture   www. paontheweb.com

Pennsylvania Department of Agriculture   www. agriculture.state.pa.us

Pennsylvania Department of Fish & Boat Commission   www. fish.state.pa.us

Pennsylvania Dutch Designs; Rebecca McKillip; Stemmer House Publishers; 1983.

Pennsylvania Facts   www. enchangedlearning.com

Pennsylvania Farm Bureau   www. pfb.com

Pennsylvania History & Culture   www. nps.gov/state/pa/

Pennsylvania: History, Geography   www. infoplease.com

Pennsylvania of Conservatory & Natural Resources   www. dcnr.state.pa.us

Pennsylvania State Association of City Fairs   www. pafairs.org

Pennsylvania State Parks   www. dcnr.state.pa.us

Pennsylvania Visitors Network   www. pavisnet.com

Trout Streams and Hatches of Pennsylvania: A Complete Fly-Fishing Guide to 140 Rivers and Streams; Charles R. Meck; Countryman Press, 1999.

Visit Pennsylvania   www. visitpa.com

Wildlife of Pennsylvania & the Northeast; Charles Fergus; Stackpole Books; 2000.

Index

Cookbooks Published by Cookbook Resources, LLC
Bringing Family and Friends to the Table

Easy Diabetic Recipes

The Best of Cooking with 3 Ingredients

The Ultimate Cooking with 4 Ingredients

Easy Cooking with 5 Ingredients

Gourmet Cooking with 5 Ingredients

4-Ingredient Recipes for 30-Minute Meals

Essential 3-4-5 Ingredient Recipes

The Best 1001 Short, Easy Recipes

1001 Fast Easy Recipes

1001 Community Recipes

Busy Woman's Quick & Easy Recipes

Busy Woman's Slow Cooker Recipes

Easy Slow Cooker Cookbook

Easy One-Dish Meals

Easy Potluck Recipes

Easy Casseroles

Easy Desserts

Sunday Night Suppers

Easy Church Suppers

365 Easy Meals

365 Easy Soups and Stews

365 Easy Vegetarian Recipes

365 Easy Casserole Recipes

365 Easy Chicken Recipes

365 Easy Soup Recipes

365 Easy One-Dish Recipes

365 Easy Pasta Recipes

365 Easy Slow Cooker Recipes

Quick Fixes with Cake Mixes

Kitchen Keepsakes/More Kitchen Keepsakes

Gifts for the Cookie Jar

All New Gifts for the Cookie Jar

Muffins In A Jar

The Big Bake Sale Cookbook

Classic Tex-Mex and Texas Cooking

Classic Southwest Cooking

Miss Sadie's Southern Cooking

Texas Longhorn Cookbook

Cookbook 25 Years

A Little Taste of Texas

A Little Taste of Texas II

Trophy Hunters' Wild Game Cookbook

Recipe Keeper

Leaving Home Cookbook
and Survival Guide

Classic Pennsylvania Dutch Cooking

Simple Old-Fashioned Baking

Healthy Cooking with 4 Ingredients

Best-Loved Canadian Recipes

Best-Loved New England Recipes

Best-Loved Recipes
from the Pacific Northwest

Best-Loved Southern Recipes

The California Cookbook

The Pennsylvania Cookbook

www.cookbookresources.com

Your Ultimate Source for Easy Cookbooks

How to Order: **The Pennsylvania Cookbook**

Order online at www.cookbookresources.com

Or Call Toll Free: (866) 229-2665   Or Mail to: Cookbook Resources
         Fax: (972) 317-6404   541 Doubletree Drive
                                                            Highland Village, Texas 75077

Please note: Shipping/ handling charges may vary according to shipping zone and method.

Please send ___ copies @ $14.95 (U.S.) each $ _____

Texas residents add sales tax @ $1.23 each $ _____

Plus shipping/handling @ $8.00 (1ˢᵗ copy) $ _____

Plus shipping/handling @ $1.00 per each additional copy $ _____

Check or Credit Card (Canada – credit card only) Total $ _____

Charge to: ☐ MasterCard   ☐ VISA   Expiration Date ⌞__⌟ ⌞__⌟ (mm/yy)

Account No. ⌞__⌟ ⌞__⌟ ⌞__⌟ ⌞__⌟

Signature _____

Name (please print) _____

Address _____

City _____ State/Prov. _____ Zip/Postal Code _____

Telephone (Day) _____ (Evening) _____

E-mail Address _____

- - - - - - - - - - - - - - - - - - - -

How to Order: **The Pennsylvania Cookbook**

Order online at www.cookbookresources.com

Or Call Toll Free: (866) 229-2665   Or Mail to: Cookbook Resources
         Fax: (972) 317-6404   541 Doubletree Drive
                                                            Highland Village, Texas 75077

Please note: Shipping/ handling charges may vary according to shipping zone and method.

Please send ___ copies @ $14.95 (U.S.) each $ _____

Texas residents add sales tax @ $1.23 each $ _____

Plus shipping/handling @ $8.00 (1ˢᵗ copy) $ _____

Plus shipping/handling @ $1.00 per each additional copy $ _____

Check or Credit Card (Canada – credit card only) Total $ _____

Charge to: ☐ MasterCard   ☐ VISA   Expiration Date ⌞__⌟ ⌞__⌟ (mm/yy)

Account No. ⌞__⌟ ⌞__⌟ ⌞__⌟ ⌞__⌟

Signature _____

Name (please print) _____

Address _____

City _____ State/Prov. _____ Zip/Postal Code _____

Telephone (Day) _____ (Evening) _____

E-mail Address _____

Enjoy the latest releases in our
American Regional Series

Classic Pennsylvania Dutch COOKING

CLASSIC TEX-MEX AND TEXAS COOKING

Best-Loved Recipes from the Pacific Northwest
Oregon, Washington, British Columbia

Best-Loved New England Recipes

The Pennsylvania Cookbook
Favorite Hometown Recipes from The Keystone State

The California Cookbook
Favorite Hometown Recipes from The Golden State

Best-Loved Southern Recipes
Home Cooking from Truly Southern Families